IRAN-IRAQ WAR

THE LION OF BABYLON
1980-1988

ANTHONY TUCKER-JONES

Pen & Sword
MILITARY

First published in Great Britain in 2018 by
PEN AND SWORD MILITARY
an imprintof
Pen and Sword Books Ltd
47 Church Street
Barnsley
South Yorkshire S70 2AS

Copyright © Anthony Tucker-Jones, 2018

ISBN 978 1 526728 57 9

Typeset by Aura Technology and Software Services, India
Maps by George Anderson
Printed and bound by CPI Group (UK) Ltd, Croydon, CR0 4YY

Pen & Sword Books Ltd incorporates the imprints of Pen & Sword
Archaeology, Atlas, Aviation, Battleground, Discovery, Family History, History, Maritime, Military, Naval,
Politics, Railways, Select, Social History, Transport, True Crime, Claymore Press, Frontline Books, Leo
Cooper, Praetorian Press, Remember When, Seaforth Publishing and Wharncliffe.

For a complete list of Pen and Sword titles please contact
Pen and Sword Books Limited
47 Church Street, Barnsley, South Yorkshire, S70 2AS, England
email: enquiries@pen-and-sword.co.uk
website: www.pen-and-sword.co.uk

CONTENTS

LIST OF MAPS IN THE COLOUR PLATES

As the war progressed Iran's U.S.-supplied weaponry, such as its M109s, became increasingly hampered by a lack of spares. (IDF)

INTRODUCTION: CHOKING WHITE VAPOUR

The survivors recalled hearing the distant roar before they saw the Iraqi jets come skimming low up the valley. The aircraft shot over the town of Halabja jerking skyward before releasing the metal burdens from their wing pylons. People fled as the first muffled explosions vibrated the ground. Those nearest fell dead instantly. There were three waves that afternoon and three the next day.

Soon the stench was appalling, as were the clouds of flies congregating over the slumped corpses. They had fallen where they stood, in their homes, in doorways and in the road, men, women and children. Death had been indiscriminate. The carnage was like a scene from the First World War, but the tell-tale broad pantaloons and droopy moustaches of the men showed them to be Kurds. The world was outraged but did nothing.

It was during the closing stages of the Iran-Iraq War in 1988 that Saddam Hussein's air force unleashed its death-dealing chemical arsenal on Halabja gassing 12,000 helpless Kurdish civilians. Saddam had invaded neighbouring Iran but failing to achieve a swift victory spent the next eight years using his superior military firepower and chemical weapons to fend off Iran's seemingly overwhelming forces. The end result was that the two countries fought each other to a bloody standstill—the Kurds dreaming of independence were caught in the crossfire. Halabja became one of the terrible defining moments of the conflict. By the time the war finished Saddam had become a self-styled absolute ruler—the Lion of Babylon who showed no mercy to his enemies.

Saddam Hussein naively assumed the overthrow of the Shah of Iran by Ayatollah Khomeini in 1979 had weakened the Iranian armed forces' will to fight. The Iran-Iraq War opened on 22 September 1980 with a three-pronged Iraqi armoured assault. In the south Saddam's mechanized columns charged into the disputed Iranian province of Khuzestan and in the centre they occupied a strip of territory from Mehran north to Qasr-e-Shirin. Later a far northern front was opened opposite Sulaymaniyah in contested Kurdistan.

There were three distinct phases to the war: Saddam's invasion, which ground to a halt by mid-November 1980, the stalemate that lasted until May 1981 and the Iranian counter-offensives that commenced from then and continued on and off until 1988. Despite the best guns money could buy, Saddam remained firmly on the defensive. Manpower was his Achilles heel and this cost him the initiative.

Officially the Superpowers stood by on the side-lines, but, thanks to the Cold War, indulged in the most appalling hypocrisy. Publicly they declared neutrality but behind

Iraq ended up using its artillery to help keep Iran's massed human-wave attacks at bay. (Author's Collection)

the scenes poured billions of dollars of weapons into the region, fuelling the fighting even further. In doing so they sowed the seeds for a much later tragedy that led to the rise of Islamic State.*

---

* See author's *Daesh: Islamic State's Holy War* also published by Pen & Sword.

1. SHORES OF THE ARABS

The ongoing row with Tehran over control of the Shatt al-Arab Waterway and Iran's Islamic Revolution in 1979 convinced Saddam Hussein that the time was ripe to act against his neighbour. The 200-kilometre-long Shatt al-Arab (literally *Shores of the Arabs* or *Arvand Rud*, Swift River in Iranian) is the confluence of the Euphrates and Tigris rivers before they empty into the Gulf. It is wide and navigable and upon its western banks lay the vital Iraqi port of Basra.

Following the 1937 border agreement (designating the low-water mark on Iran's eastern bank as the frontier), Iraq gained control over the waterway, with the exception of the areas around the Iranian ports of Abadan and Khorramshahr (where the frontier was designated at the deep waterline). Vessels plying the waterway were obliged to employ Iraqi pilots and fly the Iraqi flag (again with the exception for the three Iranian ports). This essentially meant that the Iranian navy stationed in the Shatt al-Arab was reliant on Iraqi goodwill for an outlet to the Gulf. Such an arrangement was clearly going to lead to trouble, despite Iran having a Gulf coast stretching for almost 900 kilometres with several major ports.

In contrast, Iraq's naval aspirations were constrained by the size of its coastline beyond the Shatt al-Arab. Running west Iraq has just twenty-six kilometres of coast, compared to tiny neighbouring Kuwait with 180 kilometres, plus the strategic islands of Warbah and Bubiyan that dominate the estuary leading to the Iraqi port of Umm Qasr, and a large natural harbour north of Kuwait City. Again this situation was a source of constant friction.

In 1961, with Kuwaiti independence, it took the deployment of British troops to head off threatened annexation by Iraq. Although Baghdad had recognized the boundaries of Kuwait under the Treaty of 1913, Iraq's strategic requirement for establishing an effective navy could only be met by possession of Bubiyan and Warbah islands, as well as some joint territory including the valuable southern Rumaila oilfields.

Within four years of the confrontation with Britain, Iraq was demanding the islands and a chunk of northern Kuwait to provide enough space to construct the port of Umm Qasr and a railway line that would link it to the interior. Nothing happened until 1973 when two Iraqi armoured units occupied a Kuwaiti police station at Samita and troops moved onto the disputed islands. It was invasion by stealth but Arab outrage was such that the Iraqis withdrew their men. Had they waited until the Yom Kippur War was distracting world attention they may have got away with it. At the time Vice President Saddam Hussein then suggested that Bubiyan be divided in half. When no agreement was reached Baghdad began to press that it be allowed at least to lease part of Bubiyan.

Iraqi tanks waiting to go into action—Saddam's invasion caught the ill-prepared Iranians off guard. (via Author)

In 1978 Izzat Ibhrahim, Saddam's deputy, visited Kuwait to make Iraq's strategic thinking clear, stating, 'Iraq is committed to the principle that the border should be defined in such a way that it guarantees a naval position for Iraq, securing the defence necessary for its national interests and the Arab nation's interests in the Arabian Gulf.' He suggested Baghdad rent half of Bubiyan. Two years later, with Saddam firmly in power and fearing Iranian subversion, Kuwait was to support his invasion of Iran.

It was redefining control of the Shatt al-Arab that led to the Iraq's first war with its neighbours. In 1969 after a change of government in Baghdad (which saw Saddam's Ba'thist Party come to power) Mohammad Reza Pahlavi, the Shah of Iran, revoked the Treaty of 1937. Supported by military muscle, in the form of the Iranian navy and air force, Iranian merchantmen began to ply their trade along the waterway without paying the Iraqi toll. The tiny Iraqi navy was in no position to oppose this, but in protest, in 1971, Baghdad broke off diplomatic relations with Iran and its chief ally Britain.

The Shah's plans were far more Machiavellian than just flouting regulations in the Shatt al-Arab. Baghdad then found itself the victim of an Iranian-backed Kurdish insurgency in northern Iraq in the early 1970s. The Iraqi army performed so badly, that in order to secure Iranian neutrality Baghdad had to sign up to the Algiers Agreement in 1975, which included the provision to demarcate the Shatt al-Arab waterway along the deep waterline. This was a disaster for the Iraqi navy. On the basis of the treaty the approaches to Basra were overlooked by both Iranian and Iraqi territory and Umm Qasr was in range of Iranian artillery.

Right: Saddam Hussein assumed power in 1979 and immediately waged war on his neighbours. (Iraqi News Agency)

Below: The Iranian army was equipped with the US M113 armoured personnel carrier. (U.S. Army)

However, Saddam Hussein, unhindered by Iranian artillery or antiaircraft guns in northern Iraq, again unleashed the Iraqi army on the Kurds with the desired results. By 1979 Saddam was president and demanding a voluntary amendment to the 1975 agreement on the grounds that it 'underrated' Iraq's interests. In the meantime the Shah had been overthrown by the Islamic fundamentalist supporters of Ayatollah Khomeini, who loathed Baghdad even more than the Shah. War was coming but Iraq had failed to build up its navy in time, largely because of the continued lack of anchorage.

The Kurds are the fourth-most populous people in the Middle East and one of the largest in the world denied statehood ('Kurdistan' straddles Iran, Iraq, Syria and Turkey). For a long time separatist guerrilla movements operated in Iran (KDPI), Iraq (KDP and PUK) and Turkey (PKK) seeking an independent or autonomous homeland. In Iraq they constitute some 30 percent of the total population and have a long and bloody relationship with their Arab cousins.

In September 1961 a nine-year war against the KDP's Peshmerga ('those who face death') guerrillas opened in Iraq, witnessing several civilian massacres. The two sides signed a peace agreement in March 1970, to be implemented within four years, recognizing the binational (Arab and Kurdish) character of Iraq and a self-governing region of Kurdistan. Claiming Baghdad had failed to fulfil the agreement, in March 1974 the Peshmerga, with crucial Iranian support, again took up arms.

The KDP alleged that deployment of the Iraqi army and air force units before the resumption of hostilities showed that Baghdad had been planning war since 1973. Ominously they also claimed the Iraqi government had obtained poison gas to use against Kurdish civilians, though at the time there was no recorded use of such weapons. It was during this time that Halabja was first introduced to the Iraqi air force when, on 28 April 1974, bombs killed 42 civilians and wounded over a hundred.

Intending to cut Kurdistan in half, Iraq threw 84,000 troops plus 20,000 Kurdish loyalists at a hardcore of 45,000 KDP on 20 August 1974. The Iraqi army claimed between March 1974 and March 1975 to have suffered 1,640 dead and 7,903 wounded, while the KDP reckoned it had killed 10,820 Iraqi troops and wounded another 17,400. The Kurds put their own losses at 876 Peshmerga dead and 2,238 wounded. At the beginning of 1975 they claimed to control some 25,000 square miles inhabited by over one and half million Kurds.

Disastrously for the Kurds, under the terms of the Algiers Agreement, Iran withdrew vital military support (including antiaircraft guns and heavy artillery) and the KDP's rebellion collapsed. Despite some determined resistance the KDP was forced to cease hostilities and the liberated area quickly fell back under Baghdad's control. Although the Iranian-supported Kurdish insurgency was over, a few fought on in the Zagros mountains. The KDP's pre-eminence ended with the emergence of the rival Marxist-Socialist Patriotic Union of Kurdistan (PUK) drawing support from Syria.

In neighbouring Revolutionary Iran, government forces found themselves fighting Iranian Kurdish rebels in early 1979, principal of these was the Kurdish Democratic Party of Iran (KDPI). Like Baghdad, Tehran had no intention of tolerating an independent Kurdish state and as early as 1947 had taken military action against the short-lived Kurdish Republic of Mahabad. Once Iraq and Iran had pacified their Kurds, war between the two countries became inevitable.

Above: Once Saddam and his family were firmly in control of Iraq, they made it their personal fiefdom. (Iraqi State Television)

Right: The U.S. supplied Iran with over 200 M48 tanks, some of which saw action during the Iran-Iraq War. (US Army)

Akbar Hashemi Rafsanjani, one of the Islamic Republic's founding fathers, chatting with his military commanders, 1980.

The Iranian–Iraqi border at Arvand Rud on the Shatt al-Arab Waterway. (Persian Dutch Network)

Saddam and King Hussein of Jordan inspect a captured Iranian M60. (Tom Cooper collection)

Iranian Bell 214A Esfahan. (Tom Cooper collection)

Iraqi Army Air Corps Mi-25, the export variant of the Mi-24. (Albert Grandolini collection)

2. CITY OF BLOOD

Following the collapse of the Shah's government and the resulting chaos, Saddam Hussein decided to launch a pre-emptive strike. The outspoken leader of the Iranian Revolution Ayatollah Khomeini had been calling for Iraq's Shia Muslims to overthrow Saddam's Sunni regime. Saddam planned not only to seize control of the Shatt al-Arab Waterway, but also the oilfields of southern Iran, in Khuzestan province known as 'Arabistan' by its predominantly Arab inhabitants. He hoped this would lead to a general rising against Khomeini, while pro-shahists would then issue the 'Abadan Declaration' informing Iran a new government would be formed under Prince Reza, the Shah's son, supported by his father's old officials such as ex-prime minister Shapour Bakhtiar and former General Gholam Ali Oveissi.

Saddam and his generals planned a three-pronged attack. To the north his forces were to roll over the border to attack Qasr-e-Shirin and Mehran; in the centre they would drive on Ahwaz and Dezful; while to the south their targets were Khorramshahr and Abadan (the site of the world's largest oil refinery). Probably for diversionary purposes these attacks were to be staggered (*see* map 1).

On paper Saddam's armed forces were stronger, with an army of some 200,000 troops equipped with 2,850 tanks. His air force stood at 38,000 personnel with 332 combat aircraft. The Iranian army had 150,000 men with 2,000 tanks and an air force of 70,000 with 445 combat aircraft. Although the Iraqi navy was negligible, Iran had 20,000 naval personnel with a fleet of a dozen destroyers, frigate and corvettes. While Saddam's forces were largely equipped with Soviet-supplied weapons, Iran's forces had British and American equipment that would eventually run out of spares. Saddam also counted on many Iranian units being in disarray as a result of the revolution.

On Thursday, 11 September 1980, Saddam's armoured columns struck toward Qasr-e-Shirin which lay roughly in the centre of the Iraqi–Iranian border. After taking the town the Iraqis claimed to have liberated thirty miles of disputed territory. The Iranians were slow to react and the Iraqi air force bombed Kermanshah to the southeast of Qasr-e-Shirin to deter them from mobilizing their regional militia.

Then on 15 September Khomeini accused Saddam of attempting to shoot down the helicopter transporting Iranian President Banisadr and Prime Minister Mohammad-Ali Rajai. In the meantime Iran also began to mass her border troops. Just two days later Saddam showed his hand by declaring the five-year-old Shatt al-Arab Waterway treaty null and void. In effect he was declaring war. Now fighting broke out along the waterway as both sides opened up with their heavy artillery.

There was full-scale fighting all along the two countries' mutual 720-mile frontier by 22 September 1980. The war soon spread farther afield when Iraqi aircraft bombed and strafed nine Iranian airbases. They then launched a raid on Iran's naval base at Khosrowabad to the south of Abadan at the mouth of the Shatt al-Arab. This move was to silence any Iranian naval units that might try to interfere with the Iraqis crossing of the waterway and into the Khuzestan region.

Once the Shatt al-Arab had been cleared Iraqi forces launched their full-scale invasion on 23 September. Barges were used to ferry troops and supporting tanks across from the Iraqi city of Basra to the north of Khorramshahr and south of Abadan. Farther north as planned Iraqi troops crossed the border and headed for Ahwaz and Dezful on the Karun river. At Qasr-e-Shirin Saddam's forces advanced on a front extending south to Mehran with a thrust also toward Kermanshah. Iranian forces with little in the way of heavy weaponry fell back to the towns to take up new defensive positions.

Once over the waterway, Saddam sent a column of toward Abadan six miles away. From the air his jets then proceeded to blitz Abadan, Khorramshahr, Ahwaz and Dezful. The Iranians claimed that their air defences shot down thirty-four Iraqi jets, while Iraq claimed a score of sixty-seven enemy aircraft. By the following day, the now-ablaze Abadan was surrounded by Iraqi armour and Khorramshahr was being attacked from the north. Contrary to expectation Iranian resistance did not collapse.

By 26 September 1980, fighting was still raging around the southern bridgehead as both sides poured more troops into the area. The Iraqi air force continued its offensive with strikes on six Iranian cities, including the oil port of Bushehr. In the meantime Iraqi antiaircraft batteries claimed another twenty-three kills, bringing their total up to 143, one-third of Iran's air force.

Poor Iraqi planning was soon in evidence. At the very southern end of the bridgehead an Iraqi armoured column of some 200 tanks heading east became bogged down in the salt marshes near the waterway. This was well over a divisional-strength force. The Iranians, seizing the opportunity, launched an immediate counterattack destroying eighty of the stranded vehicles before the Iraqis could retrieve them. The tank crews had little choice but flee on foot.

On 2 October Khomeini's forces launched a successful counterattack against the northern Iraqi bridgehead. They successfully retook Mehran, blocking any Iraqi attempts to move south. By 9 October, it was obvious that Saddam's offensive had already bogged down and both sides dug in. Upon surveying their gains Saddam's generals found that the northern bridgehead had taken an area twenty-five miles deep by a hundred long, extending from Qasr-e-Shirin to Mehran. The central one was slightly bigger being fifty miles deep by 120 long, extending from Dezful to Ahwaz. The southern bridgehead running from Khorramshahr to Abadan was only six miles deep.

A knocked-out Iranian BMP-1. (Tom Cooper collection)

Iranian self-propelled guns included the U.S.-built M109. (IDF)

Saddam had hoped that this would be enough to cause panic across Iran and spark a change of government. However, he grossly underestimated his enemy. With world attention focused on the war and its threat to the Middle East's vital oilfields, Saddam called for a ceasefire on Sunday, 12 October 1980. Khomeini's response was to launch airstrikes on Baghdad, Basra, Mosul and other Iraqi cities.

Saddam's invasion front was stretched over 500 miles and the war was revolving around four key battles: for Khorramshahr, Abadan, Ahwaz and Dezful. For three weeks the Iranian defenders of Khorramshahr had beaten off their attackers. The Iraqi army established its heavy artillery at Shalamcheh by 13 October, just eight miles from the city. A steady bombardment was kept up in an effort to pound the garrison into submission. Iraqi infantry fought running street battles with the fanatical Islamic Revolutionary Guard and Iranian regulars. Portions of the city continually changed hands, but the Iraqis made little permanent headway.

At one point during the battle for Khorramshahr Iranians troops bravely conducted a counterattack with little more than small arms and Molotov cocktails. Remarkably, they succeeded in driving off the Iraqis, capturing sixteen tanks and armoured personnel carriers. Finally though, tough Iraqi commandos managed to clear the streets house by house. Moving along the east bank of the Shatt al-Arab with artillery support from the west bank, they reached the mouth of the Karun river south of the city. In response the Iranians moved their tanks up to guard the bridge over the river, but Iraqi artillery fire swiftly forced them to withdraw. On 18 October Iraqi forces crossed the Karun: Khorramshahr had fallen. Iraqi units were now free to push south to link with their forces attacking Abadan.

Iranian resistance at Abadan was still holding out, even though most of the town was reduced to ruins and the refinery was pumping great clouds of toxic fumes up into the sky. Iraqi infantry attempted to surround Abadan with the aid of an artillery bombardment fired from Sieba, one mile away on the west bank of the Shatt al-Arab Waterway. Unable to clear the town, the Iraqis decided to dig in for the long haul.

Sixty miles to the north at the Iranian provincial capital of Ahwaz the Iraqis were also halted. The determined Iranian defenders, with air support, managed to keep the Iraqi armoured columns pinned down some fourteen miles west of the city. The Iranians then launched a counterattack near Ahwaz and an Iraqi regiment of 600 men were surrounded and captured on or around 10 October

Meanwhile at Dezful, the Iranian military base and oil station fifty miles north of Ahwaz, the defenders were holding up Iraqi troops that were supposed to move south to reinforce the attack on Ahwaz. Sometime in mid-October the Iraqis, in a desperate bid to seize Dezful, fired four Soviet-made surface-to-surface ballistic missiles on the town and neighbouring Andimeshk. These 6,000kg weapons caused 470 casualties, most of whom were innocent civilians. Even so, a flattened Dezful was finally captured.

Above: Iraqi officers rallying the population. (Iraqi News Agency)

Left: The Iraqi army was schooled in the Soviet doctrine of massed armoured attacks, which it sought to use against Revolutionary Iran. (Author's Collection)

Another two months of bitter but inconclusive fighting followed and by the end of 1980 none the Iraqi bridgeheads had increased in size. Both sides by this stage were firmly entrenched and the Iranians, having recovered from the initial surprise, had considerably reinforced their troops. In the face of international disapproval Saddam's anticipated spring offensive of 1981 never really materialized. Both countries though remained uncompromisingly at war and locked in a fruitless stalemate.

The fighting throughout 1981 was limited to a localized scale around the major towns and cities. No large attacks or counterattacks were launched. but the Iranians kept up an unrelenting pressure that began to bleed the Iraqis' strength dry. Both sides continued to claim victory in the south, but neither made any headway. The restricted nature of the war also gave the Iranian regulars and militias much needed time to reorganize and rearm.

By 1982, the Iranians were in a position to be able to consider a liberation offensive to retake the lost regions of the disputed Khuzestan province. This was planned against the principal defensive points of the northern and southern edges of the Iraqi bridgeheads. Their aim was to retake Dezful and Khorramshahr. Saddam was not idle and in the meantime had massed his 4th Army Corps in an attempt to stem the pressure and possibly in preparation of renewing his own operations.

At the beginning of April 1982 the Iranians struck south of Dezful. In the battle that followed the Iraqis claimed to have inflicted 20,000 casualties on the Iranians. However the northern elements of the Iraqi 4th Corps were destroyed, losing 5,000 killed and several thousand captured. The attack at Khorramshahr was launched the following month and gradually the Iraqi foothold was squeezed smaller and smaller. In Khorramshahr itself an eight-day street battle ensued as the Islamic Revolutionary Guards tried to expel the Iraqi garrison (*see* map 2). After a fierce struggle, by the end of the third week of May 1982 battered Khorramshahr was once more in Iranian hands. The total casualties suffered by both sides, in and around the city, are believed to have been over 20,000, while the Iranians claimed to have captured 30,000 Iraqi troops. Unsurprisingly, Khorramshahr was renamed 'Khuninshar' or 'City of Blood'.

After the liberation of Khorramshahr and their defeat around Dezful, the southern Iraqi bridgehead was made untenable. After the loss of the southern corner and with the northern edge threating to collapse at any moment, there was a severe danger of Saddam's bridgeheads being rolled up from north to south. Saddam's forces had little choice but to retreat toward the Shatt al-Arab Waterway. With the northern bridgehead little more than a toehold around Qasr-e-Shirin, all that been gained by Saddam in the first two months of the war in 1980 was lost.

Saddam had taken a big gamble that he could topple Ayatcllah Khomeini. A swift, decisive victory would have made him the dominant power in the Middle East, a situation that many Western countries would have favoured. Instead Khomeini's disruptive Iran emerged once again as the key country in the region. It now seemed only a matter of time before Khomeini retaliated by invading Iraqi soil.

Right and opposite: Having fallen to the Iraqis in 1980, the port city of Khorramshahr was liberated by Iranian troops in bitter fighting during April/May 1982.

In retaking Khorramshahr, the Iranians claimed to have captured some 30,000 Iraqi troops. (Government of Islamic Republic / BBCPersian.com)

Iranian troops posing in Khorramshahr, 24 May 1982 (Government of Islamic Republic / BBCPersian.com)

3. SUPERPOWER MEDDLING

Both Superpowers, despite a declaration of neutrality, from the start pursued a dual-track policy. When war broke out they were in a similar position in that neither was deeply committed to either Iraq or Iran. Nor did they have any particular desire to see one side triumph over the other. An armed stalemate served to maintain the status quo in the region and as far as Washington was concerned served to keep fundamentalist Shia Iran in check. In addition, the approach by Washington and Moscow was partly shaped by what they saw as a 'limited' war that would rapidly burn itself out. In both capitals the advice was to let things play themselves out.

There was also a whole range of other factors that shaped the Superpowers' public and private responses to the conflict. These included ongoing Cold War tensions and safeguarding Gulf oil reserves, especially in light of Iran's geostrategic dominance over the flow of oil through the Strait of Hormuz. Ironically though, the lack of leverage in the region meant that both the United States and the Soviet Union had to manoeuvre largely within the constraints of complete diplomatic impotency. Washington had to tread carefully because of the much wider regional constraints stemming from the Arab–Israeli conflict, troubled inter-Arab relations and the recent Soviet military presence in Afghanistan.

Thanks to the Cold War, the Soviets were seen as a very real threat to the Middle East. (Author's Collection)

The war was characterized by the use of tactical rockets, such as the FROG-7 seen here and Scud missiles. (U.S. DoD)

Washington's position in the Gulf was particularly inhibited by its continued support for Israel in the face of the Palestinian situation and its stance against Islamic fundamentalism. Prior to the 1979 Revolution, the Shah of Iran had provided a strong regional ally, but he had been swept away, with the U.S. ostracised by Ayatollah Khomeini who then humiliated the U.S. with the hostage crisis in Tehran, which had caused a deep rift between both countries. To compound matters Iraq had been edging into the Soviet sphere of influence since the 1960s. Diplomatically the U.S. was hamstrung with both Iran and Iraq; nonetheless Washington was determined to force the Soviets out of the region and keep Revolutionary Iran contained.

The U.S. secretary of defence, Harold Brown, on 21 September 1980, with the situation between Iran and Iraq rapidly deteriorating to the point of all-out war, publicly set the stage by noting that the fighting had serious global implications and by suggesting that it did not serve the interests of any party. The very next day saw Saddam's invasion commence. In response President Jimmy Carter declared, 'We are not taking a position in support of either Iran or Iraq. Our only hope is that the two nations can resolve the situation peacefully.'

Greatly hamstrung by the hostage crisis, within the first four days of the war, Carter's administration made its position clear: neutrality, containment, cessation of hostilities, continued access to the Gulf and the avoidance of a Superpower confrontation.

Moscow was in a similar situation and was disliked by Iran, particularly after the invasion of Afghanistan. The Soviet Union had more to lose than the U.S. by provoking this revolutionary fundamentalist state because of its own vast Muslim population. Likewise, relations with Iraq, although previously close, which helped offset U.S.-backed Iran, were beginning to decline as Saddam sought out new weapons suppliers. Conscious of losing more regional influence the Soviets saw that it would be in their own interests to seek a speedy end to the war. Soviet premier, Leonid Brezhnev, stated in *Pravda* on 9 October 1980 'neither Iraq nor Iran will gain anything from mutual destruction, bloodshed and the undermining of each other's economy'.

With the conflict escalating, a potential economic threat loomed that would inevitably compromise U.S. neutrality: namely an oil crisis. If fuel supplies were disrupted then inevitably the price would rocket. The Gulf region contained in the 1980s some 65 percent of the world's oil reserves. When the war broke out it was supplying around 60 percent of the non-Communist world's oil. Iraq and Iran in particular provided one-sixth of OPEC's total output.

The short-term effect of the loss of Iranian oil was not likely to be serious. By the end of September 1980, there was a worldwide glut of 2.5 million barrels of oil a day (mbd). The drop to 1.5mbd from 6mbd under the Shah was not a particularly important factor for the Western powers, as over the previous two years they had reduced their dependence on Iranian oil. Although the countries that would suffer were India and South Korea as well as two Soviet bloc countries Bulgarian and Romania. In Iraq's case it provided 7 percent of the world's requirement with 3.5mbd. The loss of its output would be almost as serious as the initial effects after the outbreak of the Iranian Revolution.

Understandably the Carter administration feared that the Iran-Iraq War would spark a fuel shortage—precisely what had happened during the 1973 Arab-Israeli War—that would undermine Western economies and political unity. The U.S. in 1979 got 24 percent of its oil from the Gulf States, but had considerable resources of its own to fall back on. Shortages would affect Britain which got 12 percent of its oil from Iraq and a further 3 percent from Iran, but especially hit would be France, Germany and Japan. This meant Washington was obliged to try and exert some influence, despite its stated stance of neutrality, in order to safeguard its key Western allies.

In contrast Moscow had no reliance on Gulf oil and the only major natural resource it got from the region was Iranian gas. Even so the Gulf's oil reserves still had an economic and political attraction for the Soviets. Anything that seriously discomforted the West was a Cold War bonus as far as Moscow was concerned. Furthermore, the evident

Western dependency on Gulf oil supplies provided a useful political lever. It could be used to drive a wedge between Western Europe, Japan and the U.S. security umbrella—or at least in theory.

The strategically important Strait of Hormuz at the entrance to the Persian Gulf (or Arabian Gulf depending on your nationality), rapidly developed into a potential flashpoint for a Superpower confrontation (*see* map 3). As 60 percent of American, European and Japanese oil had to pass through Hormuz it was vital it was kept open. However, the Iranians made it perfectly clear that they regarded Hormuz as part of the war zone due to Iraqi claims on certain islands.

In light of this situation Washington feared that an armed clash with Iran over the possible closure of Hormuz could then lead to a wider confrontation with Moscow. This was the driving factor behind the Carter administration urging neutrality and containment. Nonetheless as early as January 1980 President Carter pledged to intervene militarily if the Strait were closed. But with both warring countries hostile to the U.S., neutrality in the face of Soviet confrontation was inevitable. Even so Carter emphasized, 'Freedom of navigation in the Persian Gulf is of primary importance ...'

With Iran and Iraq attacking each other's oil facilities, the U.S. was determined to ensure its policy of containment. On 26 September 1980 Washington declared it was willing to convene a conference to discuss the Strait and a Western response to its possible closure. It was apparent that the Americans were planning a naval flotilla as a multilateral rather than unilateral response which would be much more acceptable to Moscow and the Gulf States. This had the desired effect and a U.S. naval force was gathered with minimum publicity. By initially positioning this in the Indian Ocean, President Carter was able to exercise a deterrent to the widening of the war, for the time being at least.

By threatening to close the Strait of Hormuz to international shipping, Khomeini exploited its geostrategic significance to the maximum. President Reagan followed Carter's stance by stating in February 1984: 'There is no way we could stand by and see that sealane denied to shipping.' Shortly afterward Saddam Hussein announced the siege of Iran's Kharg Island oil terminal at the head of the Gulf. There was almost an international incident when the U.S. destroyer *Lawrence*, escorting a tanker through the Strait, was approached by an Iranian frigate and aircraft, both of which had to be warned off in no uncertain terms. In retaliation for Saddam's actions, Khomeini threatened to blockade Hormuz, but fortunately for the U.S. the Iraqi leader backed down and Reagan's hand was not forced.

Tensions were eased because by 1984 only 20 percent of the non-Communist world's oil passed through the Strait of Hormuz (a drop of 40 percent). Likewise, the U.S. was getting less than 5 percent from the Gulf (a drop of over 19 percent). Nonetheless, Western Europe was still importing 30 percent and Japan 50 percent of their oil from the Gulf. OPEC, though, rapidly cushioned the oil consumers by compensating for the drop in Iranian and Iraqi production.

To deter attack oil tankers are being escorted by U.S. frigates and a carrier in the Persian Gulf. (U.S. Navy)

Iraqi BMP-1 infantry combat vehicle. (U.S. DoD)

After the initial success of Saddam's invasion of Iran, Washington began to fear that an Iraqi victory might lead to civil war in Iran and Soviet intervention: Iran had a 1,500-mile common frontier with the Soviet Union. As a result the U.S. was soon tempted to abandon its neutrality and supply the U.S.-equipped Iranian army with spare parts. This was on the basis that Moscow was still supplying Saddam's forces with equipment. There was even talk of arms for hostages as the U.S. had frozen $240 million worth of military equipment purchased by the toppled Shah.

When Reagan came to power the U.S. shifted its approach slightly, which was in response to public pressure to take a firmer stand against Iranian Shia fundamentalism. Although Reagan followed the policy of neutrality, he also strengthened the U.S. presence in the Middle East, building up the U.S. Rapid Deployment Force and selling Saudi Arabia surveillance aircraft—all of which suggested the possibility of American intervention.

Due to both international and U.S. public opinion, Reagan tried to distance himself from Iran by cancelling the promise of spare parts, the release of hostages having already been secured. Rather ironically former secretary of state Alexander Haig said on 29 June 1981 that 'there would be no military equipment provided to the government of Iran either under earlier obligations and contractual arrangements [or under] as yet unstated requests.'

At the same time the neighbouring Sunni Gulf States began to pressure Washington to shore up Sunni Iraq against Shia Iran, as it was becoming clear that Saddam was losing by 1981. Both Kuwait and Saudi Arabia were fearful that the fighting might spill over their borders. There was alarm that if anti-U.S. Iran should win then it would export its firebrand Shia fundamentalism and destabilize the entire region, thereby putting the world's oil supplies at risk once more.

Iraq had been a radical socialist Arab state closely tied to the Soviet Union, but these ties had greatly diminished. During 1981 America's alignment toward Iraq was characterized by what Haig called a 'strategic consensus' to counter Soviet expansionism. Such was the rhetoric of the Cold War. While the U.S. did not sell weapons direct to Iraq, it gave tacit support to NATO ally France which supplied over a third of Iraq's military needs.

Significantly U.S. diplomatic relations, which had been broken off with Baghdad in 1967, were restored in 1984. The U.S. also provided indirect economic assistance to help build new oil pipelines through Jordan and Saudi Arabia to keep Saddam's war economy functioning.

By 1986 Washington's favouritism was becoming apparent. In July that year a U.S. official cautioned, 'We used to maintain that no one could lose this war. Now we think that if the Iraqis don't play their hand right, they could lose it.' However, Iraq in a dominant position—while it would continue to evolve away from Moscow—would also foster a leadership role in the Gulf which was something that would not serve U.S. interests.

In New York in April 1986 charges were brought against seventeen men (including four Americans and a retired Israeli general) for illegally trying to sell $2 billion worth of weapons and spare parts to Iran. Ironically, that November, it was revealed that the U.S. government had been indirectly supplying arms and spares to Iran via Israel since at least September 1985. It is almost certain that this link was much older as Israel had been supplying arms to Iran since as early as 1984, suggesting tacit U.S. approval. In addition, in 1982, Israel had traded $50 million worth of Soviet arms and ammunition that had been captured in Lebanon with Iran for oil.

U.S. meddling in the Iran-Iraq War was influenced by the fluctuating fortunes of Iran and the anxieties of America's Gulf allies. America's apparent neutrality demonstrated to Saudi Arabia in particular that Washington no longer exerted influence in the Middle East in the face of a growing Soviet threat. Notably, within twenty-four hours of hostilities commencing, Saudi Arabia was requesting help. The U.S. response was to dispatch four Airborne Warning and Control Systems (AWACS) aircraft. This ensured that the U.S. went through the motions of assisting the Saudis without provoking the Soviet Union by supplying any offensive systems. Although Reagan continued to assure America's Gulf friends of military support, Congress consistently blocked the president's efforts to supply the Saudis with manportable Stinger surface-to-air missiles.

Moscow's position proved just as problematic. In the wake of the Soviet invasion of Afghanistan, there was a marked decline in Soviet prestige in the Middle East. Inevitably Moscow's response to the Iran-Iraq War was conditioned by its global priorities and a wish to safeguard regional stability. Moscow had no desire to see either a powerful anti-Soviet or pro-U.S. state on its southern borders.

Despite its military might, Moscow's options were largely limited. Despite professing sympathy with the people's Revolution in Iran, Moscow had had a friendship treaty with Iraq since 1972. Soviet support for the Iraqis could push Iran back into the arms of the West, but failure to support Iraq would worsen Soviet–Arab relations. Like the U.S., the Soviet Union opted for continued neutrality.

Such a policy inevitably hurt Iraq more than Iran, as it denied supplies and spare parts to the Soviet-equipped Iraqi army. In 1978 Saddam Hussein had purged the Iraqi Communist Party. Although the Soviets kept it a secret to avoid damaging relations, they had withheld certain military hardware such as MiG-25 jet fighters, Mi-24 helicopter gunships and SA-9 missile systems. Saddam was not blind to the implications of this punitive measure and before invading Iran, the Iraqi minister of information had declared his country would seek weapons elsewhere and had already turned to France.

Moscow appreciated that its influence with Saddam was waning and acted accordingly. Prior to the war there is little doubt that Moscow was courting Iran and in October 1980, just after it started, the Soviets concluded a special treaty with Syria—Iraq's regional rival. Nevertheless Moscow would not have benefitted from Saddam's defeat so small-arms shipments were maintained. In 1981 the two countries celebrated the ninth anniversary of their friendship treaty and Moscow continued covert weapons shipments via Eastern Europe.

Ironically, during 1979, thanks to Western sanctions against Revolutionary Iran, Soviet exports to the country trebled. Initially the Soviets were alarmed that the U.S. hostage crisis and tension along the Iranian–Iraqi border might spark U.S. intervention. America's bungled attempt to rescue its diplomatic staff from Tehran convinced Moscow that Washington was prepared to use military force. Moscow also knew it needed to keep Iran on side because there was always a danger the revolution would spread to the Soviet Central Asian Muslim republics. Soviet intervention in Afghanistan had been partly prompted as a way of heading off such trouble.

Khomeini and his fellow ayatollahs did not welcome Moscow's overtures. They suspected that the Soviets knew about Saddam's attack beforehand, but had kept quiet hoping to profit from it. A senior Iranian government official summed up such suspicions saying, 'The Kremlin thought it could easily fill what it perceived to be a vacuum left by the eviction of the U.S. from Iran.'

On 5 October 1980, Vladmir Vinogradov, Soviet ambassador to Tehran, met Iranian Prime Minister Rajai to offer military assistance. Rajai's reply was blunt and to the point: 'Nothing you may give us is worth our freedom, independence and Islamic Revolution.' He went on to object to Moscow arming Saddam and the invasion of Afghanistan.

That same month the Soviet Union and Syria issued a joint communiqué to 'support the undeniable right of Iran to decide its destiny independently, without any interference from outside'. Moscow promised non-interference, allowing the transfer of Iranian troops from the Soviet border and permitted Syria, Libya and North Korea to use Soviet airspace to resupply Iran with Soviet-manufactured weapons. By 1982 it was rumoured that there were up to 2,000 Soviet military advisers in Iran.

However, the ayatollahs remained both anti-American and anti-Soviet, having earlier cut the flow of gas to the Soviet Union. They soon moved to purge their own communists. In 1983 the Iranian Communist Party was dissolved with eighteen Soviet diplomats expelled for spying and aiding Iranian communists. Ultimately Islamic Iran had no time for the secular Soviet Union and its godless ways. Soviet first deputy foreign minister, Georgi Kornienko, visited Iran in February 1986 to protest against anti-Soviet statements in the Iranian press and about Iran's support for the Afghan mujahedeen fighting the Soviet army. Tehran countered by complaining about Moscow's continuing arms supplies to Saddam.

Ultimately the Soviet Union played a delicate and dangerous game of trying to maintain relations with both Iran and Iraq. This meant that they pleased neither and the war simply dragged on. A Western diplomat in Moscow at the time noted, 'They say they would like to see the war end, but they're not willing to risk ruining relations with Iran to end it.'

Thanks to Cold War politics and America's distinct dislike of Islamic Iran, the Iranians found themselves with few real allies. The moderate pro-Western, Sunni-dominated Arab

An Iranian BM-21 Grad on a raft during the liberation of Khorramshahr. (Mohsen Enhesari-Kashan)

states, such as Bahrain, Jordan, Kuwait, Oman and Saudi Arabia and even once-radical Egypt, threw their weight behind Saddam Hussein. None of them wanted to see Shia Iran win. Only the radical and pro-Soviet Arab states, most notably Libya and Syria, supported Iran.

The Gulf Cooperation Council member states were so alarmed by the prospect of the war spreading that they created a multinational, rapid-deployment force some 12,000 strong called the Peninsula Shield. At the time, although their combined armed forces totalled 140,000, Iran had 1.25 million men under arms. This meant that Saudi Arabia and the other Gulf States, despite spending billions of dollars on Western weapons through-out the conflict, remained reliant on Washington to defend them.

Israel, by supporting Iran, was not just simply doing Washington's bidding. It had its own strategic reasons for backing the ayatollahs. In three Arab–Israeli conflicts Iraq had provided troops for the Arab cause. Supporting Tehran was an ideal way for Israel to punish Iraq and weaken the Iraqi military. While the Iran-Iraq War continued, Saddam was not in a position to attack Israel again. An Israel official stated, 'We hope the war will continue for another thirty years.'

No matter how onerous or repressive the ayatollah regime was, to both Superpowers Iran remained the strategic prize. There was no hiding that in terms of military, eco-nomic and human potential, Iran was the most important country in the region. While Washington and Moscow cynically jostled for position to ensure they came out on top with the victor, the bloodletting of the war continued unabated.

Iraqi OT-62, Khuzestan, October 1980. (Tom Cooper collection)

Above: Iraqi T-55s, Khuzestan, Oct 1980. (Tom Cooper collection)

Right: Iranian President Banisadr visiting the front, early 1981. (Tom Cooper collection)

A very young Iranian soldier advances through the southern marshes, behind the prone figure of his buddy, 1980. (Alfred Yaghoubzadeh Archive)

Iranian troops performing salat (Islamic prayer) at the front. (Fatemeh Navvab)

Pasdaran (IRGC) RPG operator. The rocket-propelled grenade was used extensively by both sides. (Tom Cooper collection)

4. I SWEAR BY THE DAWN

The Iraqi city of Fao was once of vital economic and strategic importance, being the country's only major port before Basra. After five years of war it was a battered shell. Although relatively isolated from the country's second city Basra and the important roads between Iraq and Kuwait, the port was still of significant value jutting out between the Shatt al-Arab Waterway to the east and the Kuwaiti island of Bubiyan to the west. The capture of Fao would provide Iran with a major victory and effectively cut Iraq off from the Gulf and place Iranian troops south of Basra.

During December 1985 Iran dispatched massive numbers of volunteers to the southern front. At least 50,000 extra troops were called up, although some estimates put the figure as high as 300–400,000. The Iranians also improved their deficient training and command structure. More importantly, they improved their amphibious capabilities south of Basra, while stockpiling small assault craft and pontoon-bridging equipment. Iran created amphibious commando units of roughly a thousand men who were specially trained for amphibious and marsh warfare. A major military road network built on earth causeways was gradually constructed through the marshes and flooded areas in the south. As a result of all these preparations the Iranians were ready to launch not just a single offensive but a whole series in January 1986 that would stretch the Iraqi armed forces to breaking point.

The Iranians were to have the upper hand from the start. By mid-1985 they had begun to infiltrate the vast marshes and to successfully dominate the waterways and low islands. The Iraqi defenders responded by trying to cut down the reedbeds and building around forty watchtowers equipped with night-vision and acoustic sensors to provide early warning of approaching Iranian boats. But these efforts were too late as they had already lost control of the marshes and the Shatt al-Arab Waterway.

In the meantime, Iran enhanced its ability to attack north of Basra and developed the ability to support a major offensive to the south of the city for the first time. Between December 1985 and January 1986 they initiated a military build-up in the southern region. They mobilized and deployed nearly two-thirds of the *Pasdaran* (Islamic Revolutionary Guard Corps), including the 25th Karbala Division, 8th Najaf-Ashraf Division, Ashoura Division and the Special Martyrs Brigade. Nearly half the regular army was also dispatched to the area, including the 81st Bakhtaran Division, 30th Mazandaran Division and the 77th Khorassan Division.

Initially these forces were deployed between Ahwaz and Dezful, a main staging area, and in particular in the Hoor-al-Azim and the Hoor-al-Hawizeh marsh regions. They were then divided into two major concentrations, one to the north of Basra the other to the south opposite the Fao Peninsula. The Iraqis mistakenly concentrated the bulk of their troops in the marshes where the previous Iranian offensives—16 and 22 February 1984: Operation *Val Fajr 6*; 1 March 1984: Operation *Kheibar* and 11 March 1985: Operation *Fatim Zahra*—had occurred. The marshes border the highway and river Tigris northeast of Basra, and the Iraqis built emplacements and heavy weapons pits every fifty metres along the highway. They then braced themselves for the coming storm.

On 9 February 1986 the Iranians launched Operation *Val Fajr 8*, a three-pronged offensive against the Iraqi 3rd Corps and 7th Corps defences. By launching their attack in several directions the Iranians were able to catch the Iraqis off balance. The assault involved up to 150,000 troops. The Iranian forces to the north of Basra launched two thrusts across the marshes. They were rapidly repulsed, but it is probable that this was only a diversion. To the south the Iranian 3rd Division and 77th (Golden) Division suffered heavy casualties as they landed on the Iraqi island of Umm al-Rassas in the Shatt al-Arab Waterway opposite Khorramshahr. The island though was successfully taken and the Iranians installed themselves in the Iraqi bunkers.

The following day, 10 February 1986, the Iranians launched a major amphibious landing over a forty-mile front, attacking at six different points. The offensive was centred on Fao, fifty miles south of Basra and thirty-eight miles from Khorramshahr. During a rainy night several thousand Iranian commandos and specially trained Revolutionary Guards slipped across the 400-metre-wide Shatt al-Arab Waterway and assaulted the port (*see* map 4).

The small Iraqi garrison was taken by surprise and offered only token resistance. The unit commanders in Fao lied to their superiors as to the severity of the situation during the initial critical attack and, as a consequence, the Iraqi high command kept their large reserve back for fear of a major thrust toward Basra. The garrison rapidly panicked, abandoning their defences and most of their heavy equipment. Iranian forces then pushed northward taking a salt-making complex, and westward toward Umm Qasr. Fao was occupied by some 30,000 triumphant Iranian troops at the cost of only 2,500 casualties, having allegedly inflicted 14,000 casualties on the fleeing Iraqis and taking 1,500 PoWs. This represented their first major victory on Iraqi territory.

Saddam and his generals were extremely slow in reacting to the growing Iranian bridgehead with their ground forces. Although the Iraqis claimed to have flown up to 335 fighter and 134 combat helicopter sorties a day, this did little to halt the Iranian advance which reached east of Umm Qasr. The Iraqi air force found few exposed targets, for the Iranians had learned from past experiences and their forces were well dispersed and camouflaged. To make matters worse the Iraqis lost between fifteen and thirty aircraft to the well-prepared Iranian air defences.

The Iraqi response was slow because they still feared they would have to counter a major attack on Basra and this gave the Iranians time to dig in around Fao. On 11 February 1986 the Iranians did indeed launch a diversionary attack twenty-five miles north of Basra. The Iraqis were still committing their reserves to a fruitless counterattack on the Majnoon islands as late as 12 February.

Once established, the ground favoured the Iranians. The Fao Peninsula was too marshy for a large-scale Iraqi counterattack employing their armour and any advancing tanks would be severely exposed when using the causeway approaches to the city. When Saddam finally threw four divisions into a counterattack on 13/14 February 1986 it was poorly organized and lacked the elite infantry trained for such operations. When the 10,000-strong Presidential Guard Brigade was committed it did no better and the Iraqis were halted, suffering 30 percent casualties.

Saddam then brought his superior firepower to bear on the Iranian positions, but the defenders were well dug in and sustained few casualties. As a result the Iraqis wasted copious amounts of ammunition, firing about 600 rounds per artillery piece per day, which totalled some 20,000 rounds a day. Iraqi tanks were also used as artillery, thus wearing out up to 200 tank gun barrels in the process. The volume of shell expenditure was so high that Saddam had to rapidly buy emergency supplies on the international arms market.

By 16 February, the Iranians had successfully occupied over 300 square miles of the Fao Peninsula, although much of it was useless marshland. They had over 20,000 troops in Fao itself and a further 85,000 committed to the general offensive. They also maintained several hundred thousand men deployed for an attack north of Susangerd. After six days of fighting Iran had suffered about 10,000 casualties and the Iraqis some 5,000.

To the southwest Iranian forces had reached the Khawr Abd Allah Waterway opposite Kuwait, possibly surrounding the remnants of the small Iraqi navy at Umm Qasr. They also captured Iraq's main air control and early warning centre north of Fao, which covered the Gulf, and eliminated the missile sites being used against the Iranian oil terminal on Kharg Island. The Kuwaiti island of Bubiyan was also occupied but the Iranians were driven off.

As the threat to Basra diminished, Iraq's counterattacks began to improve. At this stage Iran was losing at least 350 men a day and Iraq over two hundred. Iran claimed to have shot down roughly seven Iraqi fighters a day, while Iraq claimed to have shot down several of Iran's remaining F-4 fighter aircraft.

Although the Iranians had built up their forces on the Fao peninsula, to some 30,000, after 17/18 February they were pushed back toward the city. There they were forced to dig into the marshes and salt-evaporator complex to the north. The three-pronged Iraqi push down the centre and sides of the peninsula advanced very slowly in the face of fierce opposition. By 20 February the Iranians were firmly dug in and surrounded by the forces of the Iraqi 7th Corps. Little progress though was made by the Iraqi columns and crucially they failed to cut the Iranian supply route across the Shatt al-Arab Waterway, which consisted only of a pontoon bridge and boats. This meant the Iranians could continue to make good their casualties.

On 21 February Saddam at last committed further major reinforcements from his 3rd Corps sector. The fresh troops, equipment and a battlefield commander from the front north of Basra were dispatched to bolster the push. Lieutenant-General Maher Abd Rashid's 3rd Corps was moved south to join the three columns of the 7th Corps. Rashid, an experienced commander, optimistically predicted his men would turn the tide of the battle and 'soon have the Iraqi flag flying over Fao'. His forces were used to reinforce the 7th Corps' northern column which had been bogged down for a week along the main road between Basra and Fao lying parallel to the waterway (*see* map 5).

The Iraqis though could not manoeuvre as effectively as the lightly equipped Iranians through the marshes. The salt flats and palm groves greatly hampered Saddam's ability to use his much superior tank force. Thus the terrain favoured the Iranians because of their basic reliance on infantry. Iraqi engineers tried to drain the pools of the salt-evaporator complex that formed a moat in front of Fao. But as soon as an area was drained the Iranians simply reflooded it. Also the Iranians were able to reinforce their forces across the waterway with valuable tanks and artillery.

The Iraqis, even after avoiding costly frontal attacks, continued to sustain heavy losses. On 23/24 February they lost nearly two battalions. While a clumsy attempt at a small amphibious attack cost them several more battalions on 9/10 March, the equivalent of a brigade was lost trying a three-pointed attack against well-entrenched Iranians.

The following day an Iraqi Special Forces unit was wiped out trying to storm the beaches of the Fao Peninsula. It was a daring operation but ended in failure. The Iraqis' 28th and 704th brigades also suffered heavy casualties advancing on Fao in late March. Until the end of the month both sides' air activity was restricted by low cloud and rain, which greatly favoured the Iranian defence. Then, on 27 March, Iran launched airstrikes on the Iraqis' supply lines.

In the meantime Iraqi troops recaptured Umm al-Rassa Island, and the Iranians east of Umm Qasr were pushed back. The Iranian bridgehead on the peninsula was reduced to about 120 square miles and, although they had suffered 20,000 casualties they managed to keep their 25–30,000 force levels constant. The pontoon bridges over the Shatt al-Arab Waterway were kept open, but they failed to bring over extra heavy weapons, although artillery was brought forward elsewhere to shell Iraq's main airbase at Shubia near Basra.

Late on 19 April 1986 the Iraqis launched the first of two attacks on Iranian positions. The fighting took place on the road running from Fao to Umm Qasr along the southern coast of the peninsula near Kuwait. Iran accused the Iraqis of using chemical weapons, but despite this they were unable to make any headway. Also an Iranian naval force was able to resupply the peninsula during the attack. By the evening of 20 April when the attacks stopped, the Iranians claimed to have killed 1,500 Iraqis, wounded 2,600 and taken more than a thousand prisoners.

Nine days later the Iranians counterattacked, launching a three-pronged assault on the evening of 29 April. They advanced in three directions: along the road to Umm Qasr, along the road toward Al Bahar running through the centre of peninsula, and northward. Their push north was successful, driving about a mile and a quarter and capturing several square miles of territory. They killed or wounded some 4,000 Iraqi troops.

By late April both sides were locked in an intractable stalemate. The Iraqis had checked Iranian efforts to advance across the Hawizeh marshes and they controlled several positions within ten miles of Fao.

Iranian efforts received a blow when the Iraqi air force carried out a strike with 56 MiG-23 fighters on an exposed concentration of M60 tanks, M113 armoured personnel carriers and BM-21 rocket launchers near Ahwaz that were preparing to reinforce their forces on the peninsula.

A lull in the battle followed until the night of 26/27 May 1986 when the Iranians launched yet another attack. The engagement, which lasted four hours, took place on the road running northward of Fao to Al Bahar. The Iranians succeeded in destroying an Iraqi battalion, inflicting 500 casualties. Although lacking the ability to break out of their bridgehead, the Iranians retained the upper hand, especially to the north and west of the peninsula. Iranian forces had reached the Khawr Abd Allah channel running south of Umm Qasr to the Gulf in February and they claimed to have sunk a number of Iraqi vessels in the waterway. On 15 June, Iranian shore batteries engaged an Iraqi gunboat attempting to escape. The vessel was sunk with all its crew.

Saddam contented himself with containing the Iranian bridgehead, for he was not prepared to sustain the large number of casualties necessary to expel them; also, another Iranian offensive to the north was still expected. Iran continued to hold at least 300–400,000 troops ready for such an attack. Major concentrations of Iranian troops were poised to launch themselves toward the strategically vital Basra–Baghdad Highway 6 across the Hawizeh marshes, causing the Iraqi military to stay its hand.

Failure to retake Fao though was a serious loss of credibility for the Iraqi armed forces and did not reflect well on Saddam and his regime. The Iranians retained a firm grip on the city with the equivalent of at least two divisions. Iran even declared it was opening a school for its troops in the city. The continued Iranian presence raised the possibility of Tehran and Iraqi exiles declaring a rival Islamic Government of Iraq centred on Fao.

Above: Islamic Revolutionary Guards' motorcycle-mounted RPG teams proved very effective. (Tom Cooper collection)

Left: Lieutenant-General Ali Sayad Shirazi, the Iranian commander at Khorramshahr, May 1982. (Government of Islamic Republic / BBCPersian.com)

Toward the end of 1986 the Iranians resumed limited operations in the area. On 1 September 1986 they conducted Operation *Karbala 3*, which saw Revolutionary Guard frogmen capture the Iraqi al-Ummaya oil platform fifteen miles southeast of Fao. Although two days later the Iraqis claimed to have recaptured it.

Nonetheless, Saddam's reluctance to become too committed to the battle of Fao was justified, when in December the Iranians began a series of offensives toward Basra. At the end of the month they launched a limited attack to the southeast, followed by attacks to the north and south in January and in early April 1987. This meant all Iraq's efforts were directed toward defending Basra, leaving the recapture of Fao of secondary importance and the Iranian bridgehead firmly in place. The port was to remain under Iranian occupation for another year.

5. BATTERING BASRA

The beginning of 1987 witnessed some of the bloodiest fighting of the Iran-Iraq War, rightly dubbed 'the war without an end', as the Iranians renewed their efforts to take Basra. It was not only Iraq's second largest city but also its main seaport, consisting of three main areas, Ashar, Margil and Basra. The latter is the old residential area west of Ashar, the old commercial district, including the Corniche along the Shatt al-Arab, Sharia al-Kuwait and Sahria ath-Thawra. To the northwest of Ashar is Margil, strategically important as it contains the port facilities and railway station, linking the city with Baghdad.

Basra lies sixty-seven kilometres from the Gulf, 549 kilometres from the Iraqi capital, and fifty kilometres from the Iraqi–Kuwaiti border. The Tigris and Euphrates rivers converge near Baghdad and then diverge before meeting at Qurna to form the Shatt al-Arab river or waterway, which flows through Basra and on into the Gulf. The Shatt al-Arab though was littered with vessels and unexploded ordnance.

Since the end of 1980 both sides were aware, that apart from military exhaustion, which after almost seven years of fighting seemed no nearer, a change of leadership was the only factor that might bring the struggle to a close. However, Iran's ayatollahs promised to end the war by force of arms. Both sides continued to wage an air campaign against each other's cities and oil facilities, but neither side's morale had broken nor had economic strangulation proved successful. The Iraqis in particular had launched some spectacular airstrikes, but Iranian oil continued to flow.

The capture of Basra raised the spectre of a rival Islamic Republic of Iraq and the military–political backlash could have resulted in President Saddam Hussein being overthrown. The full extent of how close Iran came to success only becomes apparent when examining the bloody battle for Basra, that also graphically illustrates how both countries continued to sustain appallingly high loses in what had become largely an infantryman's war.

Iran conducted a limited surprise offensive across the Shatt al-Arab Waterway on 25 December 1986, seizing the island of Umm al-Rassas, southeast of Basra. Two days later Iraq counterattacked successfully recapturing the island. This though was just a taste of things to come. Tehran launched 35,000 troops in an offensive north and south of Basra on 9 January 1987 with Operation *Karbala 5*. This severely mauled the Iraqi 3rd Corps, destroying four brigades and four reinforcement battalions. The Iranians penetrated the Iraqi defences at Shalamcheh to a depth of three miles and at Kushk and Fish Lake one mile by three (*see* map 6).

The Iraqis were reasonably quick to react and counterattacked just three days later with their Presidential Guard and 7th Corps but were repulsed. The Iranians followed this up on 13 January launching an overnight attack advancing a further two miles toward Basra, inflicting a thousand Iraqi casualties. The Iraqis were accused of using gas in their efforts to stem the Iranian tide.

Iran also launched a diversionary offensive a day later, attacking the Sumar Heights on the central front eighty miles northeast of Baghdad, liberating forty square miles with *Karbala 6*. On the southern front the pressure was kept up with the capture of Fish Lake northeast of Basra; while to the southeast at Shalamcheh the Iranians advanced four miles. A second attack on the Sumar Heights was repulsed by the Iraqis.

Five Iraqi counterattacks launched at the Sumar Heights on 15 January 1987 were defeated with the loss of 1,500 casualties. Iraqi aircraft and helicopters supported by army units attacked Iranian troop concentrations east of Basra, destroying 218 vehicles and twenty-one boats. Also on the southern front three Iraqi brigades were trapped on Bovarian Island (south of the Shalamcheh border area, twelve miles southeast of Basra) and the Iraqi tactical army headquarters east of Basra was knocked out by a surface-to-surface missile. The Iranians then succeed in seizing most of Bovarian Island and inflicting 3,000 casualties on 16 January. The following day the Iranians made another attack on the central front, being repulsed with the loss of two brigades.

Basra was now under attack from three directions: to the northeast below the artificial Fish Lake, from the east at Shalamcheh and from the southeast in the Shatt al-Arab Waterway islands. The Iranians managed to capture two islands southeast of Basra's suburbs, though Iraqi defenders on Bovarian were still stubbornly holding out. The Iraqis claimed to have repulsed three attacks east of Basra and total casualties by 18 January reportedly stood at an appalling 17,500 Iraqis and 20–30,000 Iranians. A day later Iran's Operation *Karbala 5* Phase II, reached the river Jasim just six miles from Basra, inflicting 2,000 casualties. They then dug in on the west bank and were poised to capture four islands southeast of the city. Iraqi casualties were reported at 29,000.

On 21 January Du'aija east of Basra was captured, with the Iranians inflicting 1,500 Iraqi casualties and capturing thirty PoWs. Two Iraqi attacks on the southern front were repulsed. While far to the north the Iranians also launched a hit-and-run raid on the Kurdish front, inflicting 250 casualties and routing a battalion from the Iraqi 2nd Corps in the hills near Khaneqin.

Although the Iranians were digging in on the banks of the Jasim, they still had to pierce Basra's outer defences. In late January they renewed their three-pointed push west of the river, Fish Lake and Shalamcheh, inflicting 2,000 Iraqi casualties and capturing seventy, but they could not penetrate Basra's tough defences. By now the Iraqis were beginning to fear the worst and, on 3 February 1987, launched a counterattack east of Basra but were beaten off. The day afterward a desperate Saddam called a general staff meeting to assess the deteriorating situation.

The Iranians, determined to clinch victory, dispatched more troops to the southern front. On 22 February they mounted a surprise attack, continuing the *Karbala* offensive on the road to Basra west of the Jasim and inflicting 4,000 Iraqi casualties. To the far north things there were also going badly for Saddam. Operation *Ya Allah*, commenced by the Iranians on the Kurdish front, succeeded in destroying the Iraqi 5th Corps HQ in the Diana region northeast of Erbil, killing 1,500 troops.

At the cost of 90,000 casualties the Iranians had penetrated twelve miles, seized three islands and inflicted 33,000 Iraqi casualties to date in the brutal battle for Basra. It was now time for the decisive blow. Iran was holding 200,000 troops in reserve in the Khorramshahr area and was claiming its aim was not the capture of Basra but the total destruction of the Iraqi army. Basra had become Saddam's Stalingrad.

On 29 February/1 March 1987 in an overnight attack the Iranians captured strategic areas east of Basra, destroying four Iraqi brigades, forty-five tanks and captured fifty prisoners and large quantities of ammunition. During early March heavy Iranian attacks on the southern front involving Islamic Revolutionary Guards, regular infantry, armoured units with artillery support, captured a series of crescent-shaped defensive lines east of Basra, causing a further 3,400 casualties. Also an Iranian night offensive on the Kurdish front, in the Hajj Omran area, captured Iraqi mountain fortifications, destroying one battalion and mauling two brigades.

Iran's new attack west of Fish Lake and the Dual Canal, Operation *Karbala 8*, was initiated on 6 April 1987. It penetrated to a depth of a mile, causing 2,600 Iraqi casualties and knocking out dozens of tanks and armoured personnel carriers. The Iraqis claimed to have repulsed the assault. The Iranians though were still six miles from the city. Two days later in fighting east of Basra the Iraqis lost 1,500 men, bringing their total up to over 4,000 for that period. While Iraq claimed to have counterattacked, the Iranians claimed to have pushed a further mile west of the Dual Canal and overrun two Iraqi brigades HQs (*see* map 7).

Probably largely like *Karbala 6*, designed as a diversionary operation to fix Iraqi forces and prevent them reinforcing the southern front, *Karbala 9*, appropriately launched on 9 April 1987, attacked on the northern front at Qasr-e-Shirin. Iraqi counterattacks in the area recaptured all lost territory 110 miles northeast of Baghdad, causing 1,500 Iranian casualties in twenty-four hours of fighting.

In the meantime Saddam claimed to have successfully held *Karbala 8* on the southern front, inflicting 7,000 casualties and destroying four Iranian divisions. However, Tehran claimed to have broken through a horseshoe-shaped defensive line west of Fish Lake, inflicting 3,000 casualties (bringing the total up to 7,000), taken a hundred prisoners, destroyed remnants of three infantry brigades and disabled four mechanized brigades. Iraqi commandos launched a counterattack but were beaten off, while Iraqi helicopters were accused of dropping chemical bombs west of Fish Lake

On 10 April a new Iranian thrust on the central front, possibly the Sumar area, liberated Iraqi-occupied territory (*see* map 8). Again this was probably a diversionary operation. On the southern front the Iranians seized a strategic road linking east Basra to the main Baghdad highway, inflicted over 1,000 Iraqi casualties and destroyed three Iraqi command posts. Iranian aircraft also attacked Iraqi troop concentrations and supply bases. There was now a danger of the three Iraqi army corps defending the Basra zone being cut off. Iraqi aircraft were accused of bombing Khorramshahr with chemical weapons.

A number of trends emerged in the later fighting for Basra. The Iranians showed an improvement in infantry tactics, antitank, antiaircraft and amphibious capabilities. Although their troops were still just as willing to die for the *jihad* (holy war), Iranian manpower was not being wasted on quite such a massive scale as previously. In fact the bulk of their forces had been held in reserve, with initially only a third of the troops on the southern front being committed to the battle.

In sharp contrast the Iranian air force, despite continuing attacks on Iraqi installations, seemed to have had little effect on the course of the fighting. The Iranian navy appeared to spend most of its time harassing oil tankers in the southern reaches of the Persian Gulf, occasionally engaging the few remaining Iraqi naval vessels to the north.

The Iraqis, although their defences held, were in an increasingly difficult position. Denied the initiative and necessary manpower, they continued to rely on superior firepower which could not be expected to last indefinitely. Iraqi defenders fought stubbornly, but their aggressive counterattacks were usually localized and lacked follow-up forces, in many instances their success rate was poor.

Crucially, despite improving Iranian air defences, the Iraqi air force continued to maintain mastery of the sky. It waged a particularly successful campaign against Iran's oil facilities, and a rather wasteful campaign against Iranian cities. The Iraqi air force's ground support seemed to be improving with a number of especially successful attacks on Iranian troop and armour concentrations. The largely negligible Iraqi navy was for a time trapped in the port of Umm Qasr. The Iraqi use of chemical weapons was possibly a sign of growing desperation, or simply a way of trying to maximize their kill ratio.

By mid-April, operations *Karbala 8* and *9* had come to a halt. On the southern front the Iraqis lost some 12,000 men. The Iranians claimed to have achieved their objectives, while the Iraqis claimed to have expelled them from their few footholds. Both sides had fought each other to a bloody standstill with the Iranians reportedly still six tantalizing miles from Basra. Despite their initial success they were no nearer to seizing the city, having inflicted in total over 45,000 Iraqi casualties at a cost of 100,000 Iranians during *Karbala 5* and *8*.

Ali Khamenei addresses the Basijis, 1987.

Islamic Revolutionary Guards cheering an IRIAA AH-1J, 1987 (Tom Cooper collection)

Saddam, sensing Iran's forces were spent, seized the initiative and on 17 April 1988 liberated Fao with Operation *Ramadan Mubarak*. The Iranian garrison, once 30,000 strong but reportedly down to only 5–7,000, was expelled with the loss of 200 prisoners. Then, on 25 June 1988, Saddam retook the Majnoon oilfields, destroying a force of about 10,000 and capturing a further two thousand. The bloodletting was now almost over. Essentially the victory at Fao in 1986 had been for nothing, while the battle for Basra had fatally weakened the Iranian armed forces.

Iraqi positions in the Basra area, 1986/87. Following Saddam's invasion of Iran, the Iraqi army was forced onto the defensive. (Tom Cooper collection)

Left: Islamic Revolutionary Guards with a captured Iraqi BMP armoured fighting vehicle, Basra area, 1987. (Tom Cooper collection)

Below: An Islamic Revolutionary Guards armoured column, 1987. (Albert Grandolini collection)

Above: Iranian Basiji troops being briefed before an attack. (Tom Cooper collection)

Right: Iranian troops dug in at the front. (Commandernavy)

Iranian civilians packing rations in a mosque for the troops at the front.

6. TANKS GALORE

At the start of the war the two sides threw their sizeable tank forces at each other. However, what started as an Iraqi armoured blitzkrieg soon bogged down into a war of attrition in which neither side showed any great flare with the employment of their armour. As the war progressed the Iranian army became increasingly reliant on infantry as did the Revolutionary Guard Corps.

On paper Iran had a very large tank fleet of about 2,000 vehicles, most of which had been purchased from Western sources, although the Shah was beginning diversification. Before the revolution Iran ordered 875 British-built Chieftain Mk 5Ps and 1,200 *Shir Irans* ('Persian Lion', the Challenger using Chobham armour), but did not receive the latter. The Iranians began the war with 707 Mk 3/3P and Mk 5/5P Chieftains, 187 improved Chieftains and 40 Chieftain Armoured Recovery Vehicles (ARVs). Initially Iran was also equipped with 250 British Scorpion light tanks. Those vehicles supplied to hot countries had specially fitted air conditioning as temperatures could reach up to 80°C inside. They also had a hundred British Fox and Ferret scout cars.

The Iranian army was equipped with the British-built Chieftain tank. (Royal Armoured Corps)

Saddam deployed the Soviet-built FROG-7 rocket to deliver chemical weapons. (Author's Collection)

In addition the Iranians had a considerable number of American-built tanks including 400 M47s and 240 M48s. The 90mm-armed M48, like its predecessors, was undergunned and had many design faults. The better armed 105mm M60A1 helped rectify this imbalance and in 1980 Iran had 460 of them. The Iranian army also deployed a number of American self-propelled guns including the 175mm M107, the 155mm M109 and the 8in howitzer (203mm) M110. Iran's mechanized and motorized units were equipped with 2,000 armoured personnel carriers (APCs) consisting of the U.S. M113, one of the most widely used armoured fighting vehicles (AFVs) in the world, and the Soviet BTR-40/60/152 series.

Despite this very impressive inventory, the Iranians lacked trained crews and mechanics, meaning that large numbers of these vehicles were held in storage. Armoured corps officers were persecuted for their loyalty to the Shah and their Western attitudes. Many had undergone British and American training.

Saddam commenced the conflict with 2,850 tanks including fifty Second World War-vintage T-34s and 1,850 T-55/T-62s. The T-55, derived from the famous T-34, was armed with a 100mm and easily outgunned the U.S. M40 series. The Iraqis also deployed its successor, the 115mm-armed T-62 and had fifty of the newer T-72s, although this number steadily rose. Saddam then turned to France, buying the French *Char de Combat* AMX-30 main battle tank (MBT), which was supplied to Libya and Saudi Arabia. Iraq also purchased the French self-propelled gun *Cannon Automateur de 155mm* GCT, mounted on the AMX chassis. Both Iraq and Iran used the Chinese Type 59 (copy of the Soviet T-54/55) and Type 69 (copy of the Soviet T-55) tanks.

Other light AFVs in the Iraqi armoury included the Soviet PT-76 amphibious, reconnaissance and air portable tank, of which Iraq had about a hundred. In total Iraq fielded about 1,900 wheeled armoured vehicles of the BTR-40/50/60/125 series as well as the tracked Soviet BMP-1 infantry combat vehicle.

Soviet 152mm self-propelled gun supplied to the Iraqi army. (Author's Collection)

Moscow supplied Saddam with Scud ballistic missiles, which he used to hit Iran's cities. (Author's Collection)

For divisional air defence the Iraqis and Iranians deployed the successful ZSU-57-2 with twin 57mm and the ZSU-23-4 quad 23mm self-propelled antiaircraft systems. Missile air defence for the Iraqis consisted of twenty-five SA-6 surface-to-air Gainful missile systems. This is a medium-range weapon with three missile racks mounted on a fully rotating turntable carried on the PT-76 chassis. It was given the credit for destroying over a third of the Israeli aircraft lost in the 1973 Arab-Israeli War. The Iraqis also bought the antiaircraft *Vehicule de Tir Roland* AMX-30, which carries two SA missiles for battlefield air defence. How much of Saddam's equipment was actually operational is open to conjecture.

Before the war Iran had about four armoured divisions, each consisting of two armoured brigades containing two armoured battalions, one mechanized battalion, one artillery battalion and an engineer company. At the time of Saddam's invasion they were only able to field a single armoured division on the key southern front. They also had two mechanized infantry divisions. By 1984, due to substantial losses and constant reorganizations, Iran had just three mechanized divisions, each of three brigades, totalling nine armoured and eighteen mechanized battalions. The following year Iranian armour strength included 300 Chieftain, 200 M47/M48A5 and 250 M60A1 tanks as well as 200 Type 59, T-54/T-55, T-62/T-72 tanks captured from the Iraqis. In 1986/7 Iran still had three mechanized divisions equipped with 1,000 tanks but it is doubtful all these could be put into action.

To begin with Saddam had four armoured divisions, two mechanized divisions, one independent armoured brigade and a Republican Guard mechanized brigade. This force had expanded by 1984/5 to six armoured divisions (each of one or two armoured and one mechanized brigade), five mechanized/motorized infantry divisions and two armoured Presidential Guard brigades. In 1985 Saddam's armoured force included 200 T-54/T-55, 1,000 T-62, 600 T-72, 400 Type 59, 200 Type 69 and 100 Romanian M77 tanks as well as the French AMX-30s. By 1986/7 his formations were down to five armoured divisions and three mechanized/motorized divisions, but he still managed to retain a powerful tank fleet of 4,500 vehicles. Only a fraction of this number though was combat-ready.

Both sides lost armour at a rapid rate and in large numbers, showing how vital replacement sources were and how this dictated the use of armour in addition to the usual terrain constraints. Furthermore, Iraq and Iran employed their armoured forces in unimaginative ways and often in a cumbersome manner. During the initial invasion in September 1980 in which the Iraqi spearhead consisted of mixed armoured units, they ended up with several hundred tanks and APCs stranded south of Abadan.

The lack of Iranian air cover was notable from the start: on 12 October 1980 the Iraqis used pontoon ferries to get their tanks across the Karun river north of Abadan with little or no interference from the Iranian air force. It was only when the Iraqis became embroiled in Khorramshahr that they lost more APCs. Even with the Iranian counter-offensive in 1982 Iraqi armour was still able to use the Khorramshahr highway with impunity.

By February 1983 Iran had captured 1,460 Soviet tanks and APCs, many of which they were able to recondition through the acquisition of Soviet engines. The Iraqis, though, always managed to obtain adequate replacements. At the beginning of June 1984 Iraq deployed hundreds of tanks on the southern front in anticipation of an Iranian offensive, including T-72s some apparently on brand-new tank transporters. They lost forty-five tanks and APCs, mainly to Iran's Chinese-manufactured recoilless rifles and Soviet rocket-propelled grenades (RPGs), during the Iranian Operation *Fatim Zahra* and the battle for Highway 6 north of Basra in March 1985.

Fear of Iranian antitank weapons resulted in another sixty Iraqi tanks on the same front forming a laager, despite the fact they had the upper hand. The Iranians seem to have had an abundance of RPGs and the Iraqis captured large numbers, including one batch of over 34 launchers. This may be accounted for by the fact that in 1978 the Shah's government was operating an RPG-7 factory and it was still producing in March 1982.

In December 1985 the Iranians amassed assault craft and pontoon-bridging equipment ready for their assault on the southern Fao peninsula, dubbed Operation *Val Fajr 8*, on 9 February 1986. During the offensive Iraqi air support was poor; their air force found few exposed targets as the Iranians had learned from past experiences the importance of

Iraqi Cascavel armoured car—this was a Brazilian design. (U.S. NARA)

Battery of Iraqi self-propelled SA-6 surface-to-air missiles. (U.S. DoD)

dispersing and camouflaging their forces. As mentioned, after the failure of their counter-attack on 13/14 February 1986, the Iraqis used their tanks as artillery, wearing out several hundred tank gun barrels in the process. The Iraqi air force failed to cut the pontoon bridges over the Shatt al-Arab Waterway, and the Iranians were able to reinforce their bridgehead with their own tanks and artillery.

When the Iranians recaptured Mehran during *Karbala 2* on 2 July 1986 the Iraqis lost at least twenty armoured vehicles. During the Iranian offensive *Karbala 5* in January/February 1987, their acquisition of large numbers of U.S. antitank weapons cost the Iraqis more than ninety-five tanks and APCs. On 7 April 1987 the follow-up Operation *Karbala 8* destroyed dozens more Iraqi AFVs. Sensibly, Iraq had reportedly kept her aged T-34 tanks back in the defence of Baghdad.

Iranian use of armour was notoriously bad, and compounded by a lack of air cover this was exacerbated by the resupply problem. For example thirteen Iranian tanks were knocked out by an Iraqi helicopter strike near Susangerd on 19 November 1980. By the end of 1980 the Iraqis had captured thirty-one Chieftains, twenty-five M60s and forty-three assorted AFVs, many of which were collected together in a large vehicle park in Baghdad and put out on display.

In January 1981 during an abortive counterattack south of Susangerd the Iranians lost a hundred tanks, while in September that year, during Operation *Thamin Ul-A 'imma*, in which the Iranians lifted the siege of Abadan, they lost 150 of their M48A5s that were simply abandoned. This was probably down to poor crew training. Ironically, in 1987, they brought the tanks back off the Iraqis, who were unable to integrate them with their Soviet equipment, through a middleman in the Emirates. Another 196 tanks were lost on 22 March 1982 in Operation *Fath Ul-Mobin* launched west of Dezful and Shush.

The replacement of war losses was a problem for both sides, and new arms had to be secured from a variety of sources. In February 1981 reports from London and Washington indicated Iraq had received about a hundred T-55s from the German Democratic Republic or Poland via Saudi Arabia. To circumvent the U.S. arms embargo Iran turned to a number of Eastern and Western European countries, as well as Israel, Syria, Libya and North Korea. In July and October 1981 Israel sent tank spares and ammunition for Iran's U.S.-supplied equipment, while on 14 July 1981 Libya began shipment of 190 vitally needed replacement tanks after training 200 Iranian tank crew members. Also in July there were indications that a Soviet–Iranian agreement had been reached over training officers and providing technicians.

After successfully expelling Iraq's invading forces, Iran needed arms on a systematic basis, as ad hoc supplies were severely hampering the effectiveness of its operations. In February 1982 Iran made it clear that it would accept Soviet weapons and advisers. Syria's role as a middleman was enhanced and that March the volume of arms through Syria increased, including Soviet engines for captured Iraqi tanks.

In the U.S. the government turned a blind eye to private companies exporting spare parts to Iran. One American company regular sent goods marked 'Tractor Engines' from Boston to Tehran. This continued until a customs officer with military background noticed the engines were equipped with superchargers. They were being used as replacements for the engines in Iran's M60s. By the end of 1982 North Korea had supplied Iran with 150 T-62s. In 1985 the Iranians ordered a hundred tanks from Argentina and 200 from China that was also supplying Iraq with Type 69s.

Initially the Soviet Union ceased its arms shipments to Iraq, but the Iraqis simply turned to France. By the end of 1980 Iraq had acquired more than a hundred AMX-30 tanks and scores of light armoured cars equipped with SS-11 antitank missiles. During 1985/6 France was still supplying Iraq which took delivery of eighty-five 155mm GCT self-propelled guns, eighteen antiaircraft Roland 2 systems and AMX-30 armoured recovery vehicles. The U.S. exchanged weapons with Iraq for four years despite the policy of neutrality. Pentagon officials are said to have negotiated as far back as 1982 to swap 175mm artillery for Soviet helicopters and armoured vehicles.

Tactical use of tanks on both sides was poor. Regardless of the unfavourable terrain, neither side seemed able to effectively organize and conduct large-scale armoured operations. When Iraq first invaded Iran its armoured formations, schooled in Soviet doctrine

Iraqi T-62, Khorramshahr, November 1980. (Tom Cooper collection)

and led largely by British-trained officers, did exhibit blitzkrieg characteristics. The Iraqis used large columns of up to a hundred tanks, which in one instance were moved around on tank transporters because of the unsuitable roads. But lacking infantry support, particularly those trained for street fighting, the invasion bogged down round the cities and nothing came of their opening armoured thrusts. Coordination and cooperation between infantry and armour on both sides was poor.

Iran's armour usually operated as independent brigades in support of regular army, *Pasdaran* (Islamic Revolutionary Guard Corps) and *Basij* (Popular Mobilization Army) operations. Inter-service rivalry and poor communication between these organizations greatly hampered effective planning, with predictable results. Increasingly the Pasdaran and Basij relied on massed human-wave attacks using teenagers to capture their objectives. The army's commanders were understandably horrified by the resulting loss of life.

Iraqi air power made it difficult for the Iranians to operate effectively even on a divisional level. Iran, without adequate air cover, could not concentrate its armour, nor did it ever have sufficient numbers to do so. The Iranians proved particularly inept in the tactical siting of their tanks, which resulted in them being easily knocked out. Most of Iraq's armoured divisions ended up committed to static defence roles near Baghdad and Basra. Generally both sides resorted to using their tanks as mobile artillery or pillboxes.

7. BEIJING, MOSCOW & PARIS HELP OUT

The war was an incredible bonanza period for the major arms manufacturers. Initially either side's traditional suppliers, the U.S. and the Soviet Union, declared neutrality and refused to supply any additional weapons. Neither Iran nor Iraq were in the least bit hampered by this; in fact the Iraqi air force was able to amass an array of modern hardware that became the envy of the Middle East.

While Iraq imported weapons from some two dozen countries, three important culprits stand out, each of whom had a significant impact on the development of the Iraqi air force. Between 1980 and 1990 more than half of the conventional arms exports to Iraq came from three of the five permanent members of the UN Security Council. The Soviet Union accounted for over half with 55 percent, France with 19 percent and China 8 percent. Crucially it was France and Russia who assisted Saddam to escalate his attacks on Iran's cities and oil tankers and deliver his chemical weapons.

Major Iraqi Weapons Imports 1980–89

Supplier	Value in $ billion	% of total
Brazil	1.067	4
China	2.261	8
Czechoslovakia	0.593	2
Egypt	2.0	4
France	5.076	19
Soviet Union	15.6	55
Others	2.262	8
Total	28.859	100

During the mid-1980s Saddam's air force received a steady stream of equipment including Brazilian Tucano, Chinese F-7, French Mirage F-1 and Russian MiG-23/25/29 aircraft as well as Italian AB-212, A-109 and Russian Mi-24 helicopters. Inevitably deliveries of highly sophisticated aircraft and missiles enabled Saddam to expand the strategic scope of his war by attacking Iran's vulnerable oil infrastructure and civilian population.

After the Soviet–Iraqi Treaty of Friendship and Co-operation was signed in 1972, Moscow provided the backbone of the Iraqi air force, including 115 MiG-21, eighty MiG-23, sixty Su-7, thirty Su-20, twelve Tu-22 and Il-28 aircraft (though ten of the MiG-21s may have come from the Sudan). The Iraqi air force's initial need for more weaponry was fuelled by a renewal of the Kurdish insurgency in the mid-1970s. Subsequently Saddam Hussein damaged relations by purging the Iraqi communist party: as far as he was concerned, his position as president was more important. Although the Russians kept it quiet to avoid a showdown, they withheld certain supplies such as MiG-25 fighters, Mi-24 gunships and SA-9 missile systems.

Paris, with an eye on lucrative Iraqi oil contracts, proved to be a willing alternative arms supplier. For thirty-five years French defence industries and military procurement policy operated under the assumption that arms exports complemented national security. Foreign sales helped finance its completely independent arsenal that operated outside NATO. Although the Iraqi–French relationship began back in the late 1960s when Baghdad had expressed an interest in the Mirage III, things did not really begin to develop until the 1970s.

Paris placed a proverbial foot in the door in 1977 when Iraq signed for thirty-six Dassault Mirage F-1s and four F-1B trainers. France was relieved by this deal as Egypt had wavered over a similar one for 200 F-1s, a contract Dassault could ill afford to lose. Several years later they were followed by another deal for Gazelle, Lynx and Puma helicopters for the Iraqi air force and Iraqi Army Air Corps. In early 1980 Iraq bought another batch of 24 F-1s, took an option on the newer Mirage 2000 and negotiated the purchase of the Crotale air defence systems.

In total the Iraqi air force contracted for approximately 130 Mirage F-1s with the final batch of twenty-eight costing $500 million ordered in 1986. Dassault, despite evaporating foreign orders, was able to delay restructuring through continual replacement orders for the Iraqis (approximately two dozen annually). It finally came unstuck with the imposition of the UN embargo in 1990, which stalled a 1987 order for another sixteen aircraft. Other French defence companies also fared well because of France's role as Iraq's principal supplier of advanced weaponry. For example, Aerospatiale's highly successful helicopters were France's biggest export product by the late 1980s.

French deliveries between 1980 and 1987 were estimated at $5–9 billion, making it one of the largest suppliers to either side. According to American figures, this mantle was actually taken by China in the early stages of the war, providing $3 billion worth of arms to Iraq between 1981 and 1982 (and another $1 billion to Iran for that matter). Russian supplies were thought to amount to $2–7 billion, while Egypt provided another $2 billion in the same period. Between 1979 and 1983 the CIA estimated that Iraq received a whopping $17.6 billion worth of arms from all sources.

In order to help Baghdad's war effort France even agreed to lease its latest state-of-the-art strike aircraft. This was to cause panic among the shipping lanes of the Gulf, but fortunately

Saddam obtained over 100 Dassault Mirage F1s during the 1980s. (U.S. Defense Imagery)

Iraqi antiaircraft artillery—the Soviet designed S-60 57mm gun. (U.S. DoD)

was not as decisive as feared. In October 1983 Iraq received, on special terms, five French Super-Etendard fighter-bombers capable of carrying the feared AM-39 Exocet antishipping missile, which had made such a name for itself during the Falklands conflict.

Things really cranked up in January 1983 with the signing of a deal worth $2 billion that included, among other things, MiG-23s and MiG-25s for Iraq. During the Iran-Iraq War it was the Soviet-supplied MiG-23 and Su-22 and Soviet-trained pilots who conducted most of the Iraqi air force's chemical attacks. In March 1984 Moscow started delivery of its then new Tu-22 Blinder bombers to Iraq. The Iraqi air force also reportedly received Soviet AS-4 Kitchen and AS-5 Kelt air-to-surface missiles to go with these aircraft.

Value of Soviet arms exports to Iraq 1983–87 (in US$)

1983	1984	1985	1986	1987	Total
3bn	4.1bn	2.9bn	2.1bn	3.5bn	15.6bn

Moscow's generosity to the Iraqi air force did have limits. In the middle of Iran's 1987 spring offensive the Soviet Union apparently denied Iraq about forty-five MiG-27s and possibly some MiG-23s due to problems over payments. Moscow though did not wish to lose ground to the French and offered better financial terms to the tune of $3 billion, thereby persuading Iraq not to purchase the sixty Mirage 2000s. Also as an act of good faith Moscow offered Iraq the MiG-29, which had previously only been supplied to India and Syria. In early 1987, twenty-four such aircraft were duly delivered.

By 1984 the Iraqi air force had added three new combat squadrons to its order of battle. Nevertheless the Iraqis were not appreciative of all this equipment. In contrast to the MiG-23, which was highly thought of by Iraqi pilots, the Su-20 ground-attack fighter was deemed a real 'clunker', despite it being able to carry twice the external load of the Su-7 over a 30 percent greater range. Likewise, China's MiG-21 copies were not easy to operate or maintain and were poor performers. The Iraqi air force's MiG-25s were relegated to bomber-escort duties.

To cope with this influx of equipment the air force also created two subsidiary commands for army and naval aviation. These were allocated 140 helicopters forming six new helicopter squadrons. To begin with the Iraqi Army Air Corps was mainly equipped with Mi-24 gunships, but subsequently deployed antitank-missile-armed Gazelles, BO-105s and Hughes 500s. While the air force and air corps were generously equipped, so was the Iraqi Air Defence Command with an influx of French and Soviet systems. In particular it received the SA-2, that veteran of the Vietnam War, and the SA-6, veteran of the Yom Kippur War

Another beneficiary of the Iran-Iraq War was communist China, who by the mid-1980s was the fifth largest arms exporter in the world. Ironically, as the only state to consistently supply both sides during the war, it was able to become a major global supplier.

China adopted a policy of political even-handedness providing low-cost weapons; in particular it sold its Shenyang F-6/7 (MiG-19/21 derivatives) to both Iraq and Iran. Much of China's weapons were shipped via Egypt.

Egypt, ostracized by the Arab world after its 1979 Camp David peace accord with Israel, saw an opportunity for rehabilitation and a fast buck. Initially Egypt adopted a policy of neutrality, but by 1981 with the war swinging against Iraq the Egyptians offered Saddam military aid. Egypt, a fellow Arab state 'acted' to help defend Iraq against Iran's Persian hordes. It resulted in the largest arms transaction in Egyptian history, worth $800 million, on top of which it earned almost another $200 million as commission brokering the resale of arms from Europe. This was followed by a $2 billion deal three years later.

The Egyptians provided Saddam with not only Chinese F-6/7 fighters but also Soviet Tu-16 and Il-28 bombers. Grasping a chance to gain combat experience, the Egyptian air force loaned Saddam aircraft and pilots. Some 2,000 Egyptian advisers and technicians were to serve in Iraq. In early 1983 Egypt confirmed that forty F-6 Shenyangs had been delivered to Iraq, consisting of thirty assembled, and flown from Jordan's King Faisal airbase and ten similarly built from crated components in Egypt. The Egyptians undoubtedly provided pilots for these fighters, but China was reticent to do so as it was selling the same aircraft to Iran.

The Chinese, the French and Soviets also indulged in double-dealing by selling billions of dollars of weapons to Iran. All of it was clearly detrimental to the Iraqi air force. Iran is thought to have received several hundred MiG-19s and MiG-21s from China, North Korea, Libya and Syria, the majority of which were F-6s, despite Chinese denials.

In particular North Korea supplied some 40 percent of Iran's $2 billion worth of arms imports in 1982 and in April 1983 Iraq claimed that the Iranian air force had been supplied with F-6 jets from North Korea. Unconfirmed reports also suggested that North Korea supplied F-6 jets and SA-2 surface-to-air missiles in 1986. Nevertheless, the Iranians were apparently not very pleased with the equipment provided and North Korea appears to have been used as a last resort when other sources had dried up.

While Iran officially denied the North Korean link, in March 1984 the Chinese signed a $1.45 billion arms-for-oil deal with Tehran that allegedly included F-6/J-6 fighters; deliveries started in April 1985. Saddam cannot have been pleased when China supplied the Iranian air force with forty-eight F-6s and F-7s during 1986/7 allegedly part of a $1.6 billion deal signed in March 1985 (though this may have been the same deal as the previous year).

In total China provided Iran up to seventy F-6 fighters as well as CSA-1, Hong Ying-5 and HQ-2B SAMs. The MiG derivatives were not in evidence by the late 1980s, perhaps in part due to a lack of pilot training, though in reality an aircraft based on a thirty-two-year-old design was hardly likely to wrest air superiority from Iraq's MiG-23s, MiG-25s and F-1s. Notably, while Saddam broke off diplomatic relations with Libya and North Korea for supplying aircraft and other hardware to Iran, he did not sever them with China.

Iranian Chieftain. (Tom Cooper collection)

PR photo of an Iraqi helicopter with tanks of the Iraqi-supported MEK/MKO, 1987/88. (Albert Grandolini collection)

8. BATTLE FOR THE SKIES

Saddam Hussein's invasion of Iran was greatly encouraged by intelligence that indicated his enemy's air defences had all but ceased to function. He had every reason to believe that his powerful Soviet-supplied air force would swiftly gain air superiority. This would allow his fighter-bombers to range far and wide, that would enable him to paralyze the Iranian ground forces. Longer term, he would be able to strike at the heart of the Iranian economy by bombing its vulnerable oil industry. Certainly during the initial stages of the war in 1980/1, Iran, due to shortages of pilots, ground crews and spares, only put up limited numbers of its American-suppled F-4 and F-5 jets, although reportedly some of is F-14s were also used to effect.

Saddam's air force though was not without its problems and suffered from poor tactical strike capabilities and ground liaison. Many of his inexperienced pilots did not prove as proficient as he hoped. There was also inter-service rivalry between the Iraqi air force and the army over the control of resources. Notably, most fighter losses on both sides were caused by air defences rather than actual dogfights.

After Ayatollah Khomeini came to power in 1979, the impressive Iranian air force, once regionally second only to that of Israel's, suffered from a series of debilitating purges resulting in the loss of some 12,000 personnel. Due to the air force previously attracting

Iranian F-5 fighters—Saddam anticipated Iran's air force would be grounded. (Iranmilitaryforum.net)

Both the Iranians and Iraqis deployed the ZSU-23-4 self-propelled antiaircraft system. (U.S. DoD)

educated recruits, it was seen as a hotbed of support for the ousted Shah. As a consequence the Iranian air force was perceived as an enemy of the Islamic Revolution. It lost another 20 percent of its men through desertion, leaving it in a state of complete disarray. Following Saddam's invasion, Khomeini's purges continued throughout the armed forces for fear of royalist plots. Nonetheless, many surviving pilots had to be let out of prison to help defend their country.

The Iranian air force's morale was further harmed by having a succession of commanders, some of whom only lasted in post just days. This game of musical chairs did nothing to help its combat performance. Some idea of the difficulties arising from personnel shortages can be gleaned from the fact that in 1985 the deputy commander-in-chief, a man called Bazargan, only held the rank of airman. Taking such a job was clearly a poisoned chalice.

Quite surprisingly, in light of its overall poor condition, the Iranian air force did quite well in responding to Saddam's opening attack. Soon after his invasion, 140 Iranian aircraft reportedly bombed the Iraqi oil wells at Mosul and Kirkuk as well as the Basra petrochemical complex. This was a quite remarkable feat if the numbers are to be believed—even 140 sorties would still be impressive. With Saddam's bombing of Iran's Abadan oil refinery both sides suspended oil shipments on 26 September 1980.

In ground-attack capabilities Saddam maintained a significant superiority. Although Iran had some operational ground attack units, Iraq's easily outnumbered them.

An Iranian fighter ace with his F-14 Tomcat. (Iranian Air Force)

What was left of Bimarestan-e Susan, or Susan Hospital, Qasr-e Shirin, Kermanshah province, Iran, 1980. (Mahdi Kalhor)

The Iranians, increasingly short of functioning aircraft, were obliged to rely on helicopters for ground support. Notably flying in groups of two or three, their U.S.-built AH-1J Sea Cobras operated in the forward battle area flying nap-of-the-earth missions and providing much needed support for the hard-pressed ground forces.

Iran's air defences, despite being equipped with modern surface-to-air missiles, proved to be wholly inadequate, permitting the easy penetration of its air space. Saddam was even able to use his cumbersome Soviet T-16 Badger and T-22 Blinder bombers, armed with air-to-surface missiles, with impunity.

Saddam could also call on the Iraqi Army Air Corps which was formed in 1981; its operations against Iranian ground troops were quite successful. However, there was poor communication between the Iraqi army and air force as well as poor target acquisition. Indeed the latter was often left up to the regional airbase commanders, signifying a worrying lack of strategic planning for the conduct of the air war. In addition, the Iraqi air force felt it should control the helicopter fleet, not the army.

Due to Iraq's poor MiG-23 fighter-bomber low-level attacks, Saddam frequently had to rely on the army's Mi-24 helicopter gunships instead. The situation was only partially rectified in the mid-1980s when Indian air force low-level bombing instructors arrived to help. It was at this point that Saddam began to accelerate the Tanker War in the Gulf as a way of disrupting Iran's oil industry.

It was not until March 1985 that Saddam launched a wide-ranging, strategic bombing campaign against Iranian military and civilian targets with the intention of forcing Khomeini to the negotiating table. Air Marshal Hamid Sha'aban claimed the following month that the Iraqi air force could bomb any part of Iran at will. This was no hollow boast. Industrial and military targets from Ahwaz, Bakhterah, Bushehr, Dezful, Hamadan, Ishfahan, Rasht Shiraz, Tabriz to Urmia were all bombed. The Iranian population were left reeling, wondering where its air force was.

Tehran, with its own air defences in tatters, was regularly attacked by large numbers of Iraqi fighter-bombers, with up to two raids a day. Despite the presence of three nearby Iranian air fields, the Iraqis were able to hit all the main targets in the capital with relative ease. It was always the unfortunate civilian population who bore the brunt of these attacks, the bombs killing indiscriminately wherever they landed (*see* map 9).

Increasingly, Saddam hammered Iran's exposed infrastructure facilities. On 25 November 1986 his pilots attacked six targets including a surface-to-air missile site near Dezful and railway station at Andimeshk. This was followed by further raids on 5 December, when army barracks at Mariwan, Moshahk and Rabat were bombed. Also attacked were the Haft Tieh railway station, the Mellah Zingh road bridge and the Tshawer bridge. On the next day Iraqi aircraft penetrated as far as the Caspian

N

Qasr-e-Shirin

IRAN

Ilam

Baghdad

Mehran

R. Tigris

Dezful

R. Karun

IRAQ

Susangerd

R. Euphrates

Ahwaz

Khorramshahr

Basra

Abadan

Fao
(Al-Faw)

0   50   100   150   200 kms

Persian Gulf

Map 1: The war zone

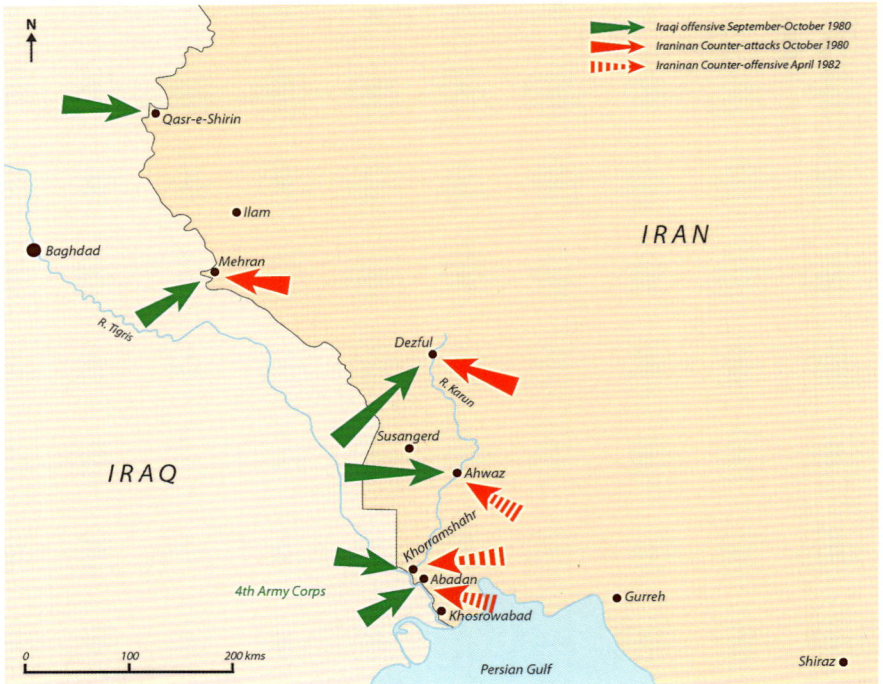

Map 2: The war, September 1980 to April 1982

Map 3: The Soviet threat

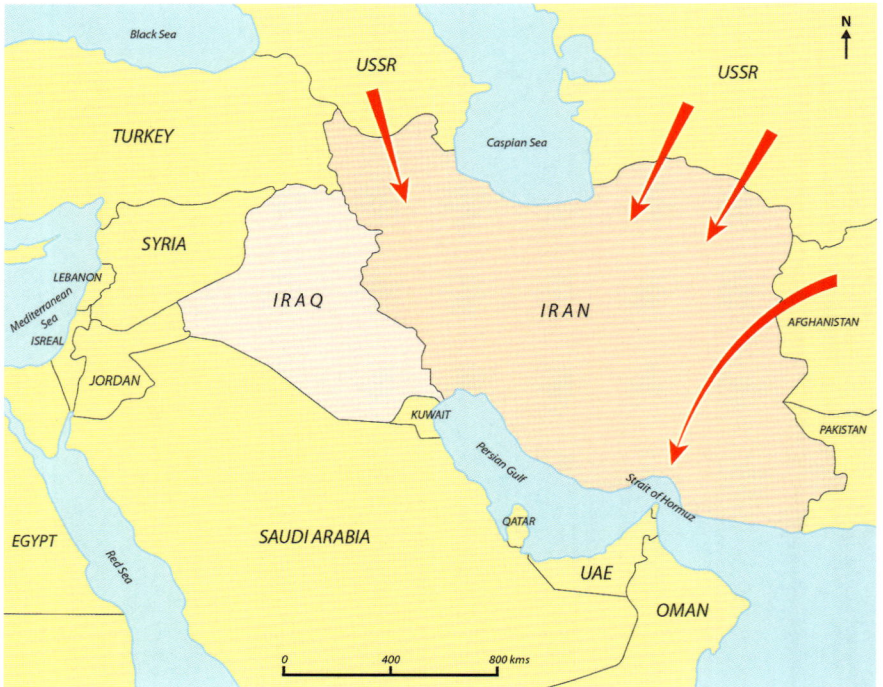

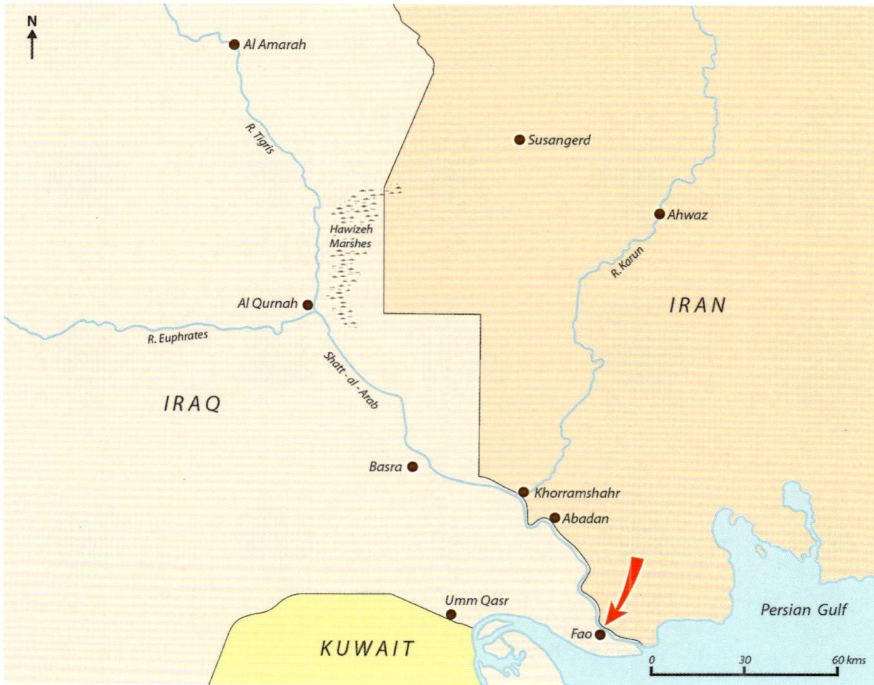

Map 4: Operation *Val Fajr 8*

Map 5: The Fao Peninsula

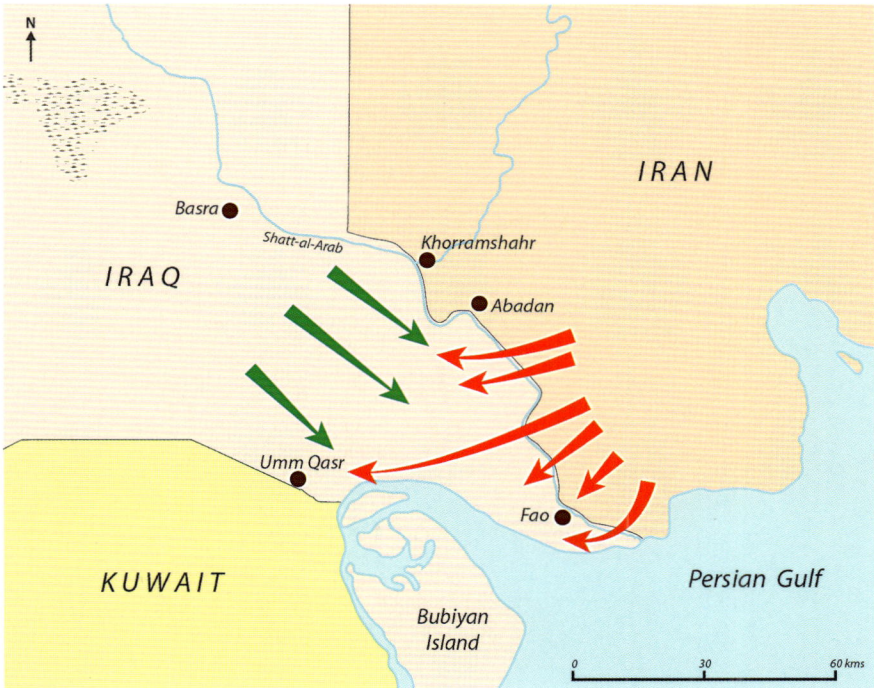

Map 6: Operation *Karbala 5*

Map 7: Operations *Val Fajr 8* and *Karbala 5* and *8*

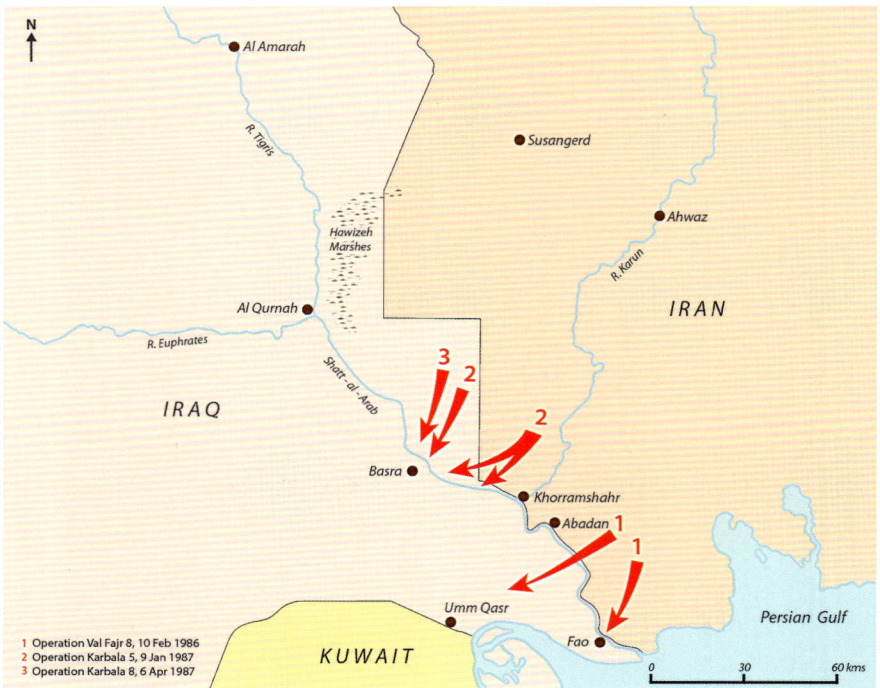

1 Operation Val Fajr 8, 10 Feb 1986
2 Operation Karbala 5, 9 Jan 1987
3 Operation Karbala 8, 6 Apr 1987

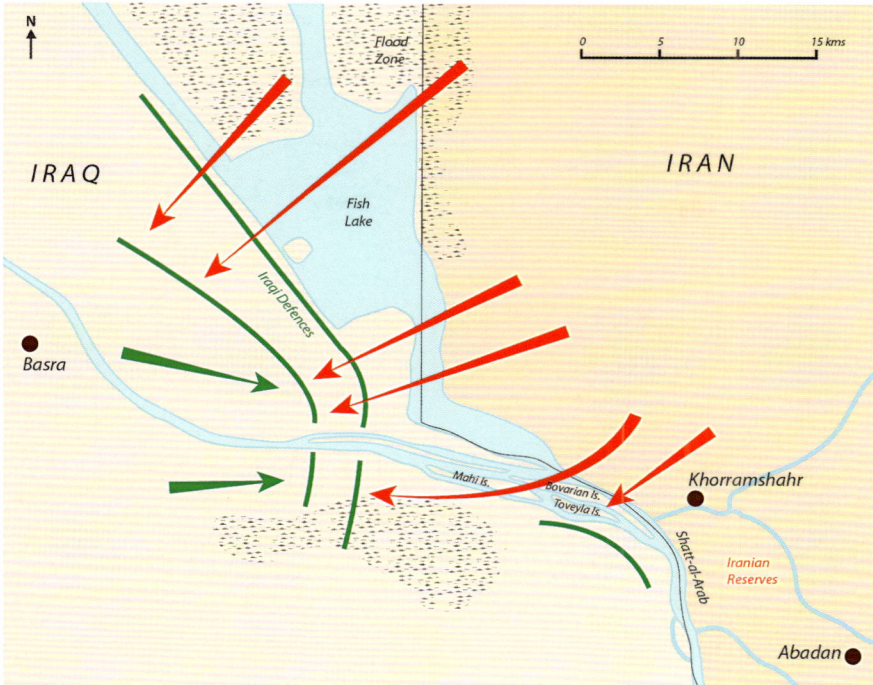

Map 8: Operations *Karbala 5* and *8*

Map 9: Range of Iraqi airstrikes

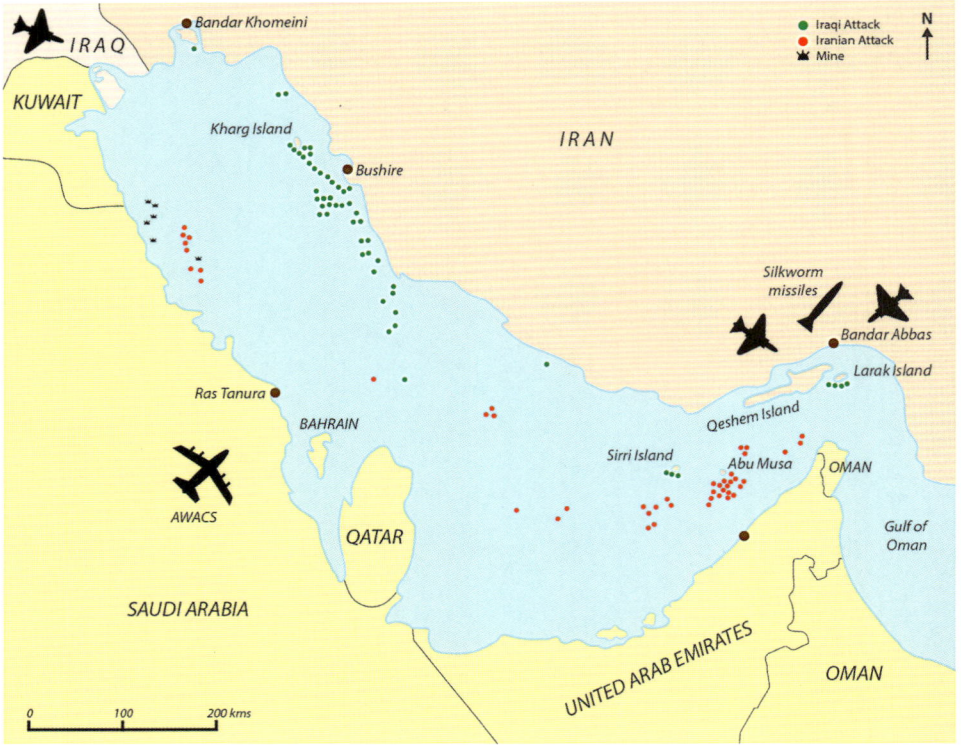

Map 10: The 'Tanker War'

A dug-in Iraqi T-55 tank, 1986. (Pit Weinert collection)

An Iranian patrol boat in the Hawizeh marshes, 1984. (Tom Cooper collection)

An Iranian BM-21. (Tom Cooper collection)

An Iranian Revolutionary Guards defensive position, 1986/87 (Tom Cooper collection)

A port quarter view of the guided-missile frigate USS *Stark* (FFG-31) listing to port after being struck by an Iraqi-launched Exocet missile on 17 May 1987. (Pharaoh Hound)

An Iranian Chieftain tank. (Tom Cooper collection)

Sea, bombing the Dangha power station. There could be no denying the reach of Saddam's air force.

Behind the scenes Tehran worked desperately to prevent these deep-penetration raids. In doing so it turned reluctantly to its arch-enemy Washington. Despite the Iranian air force's weak performance, the air defences showed some definite improvement. Between September 1986 and November 1986 Washington supplied Tehran with Hawk surface-to-air missiles which contributed significantly to Iran's ability to shoot down Iraqi jets. Certainly, during the fighting in early 1987, Iraqi aircraft losses were more substantial.

Operation *Karbala 5*, launched toward Basra on 9 January 1987, saw the Iranians using a new weapon for the first time, most probably the Improved Hawk missile system. By 14 January, the Iraqis had reportedly lost thirty-eight aircraft. This was some achievement by the Iranians in the space of just six days. Although the Iraqi air force became cautious, it still maintained mastery of the sky and on 14/15 January 1987 its pilots flew over 500 combat missions.

Then, in late January, Lieutenant Abdel Ali Fahad flying an Iraqi MiG-23 was shot down at 10,000 feet near Basra reportedly by a Hawk missile and captured. In a subsequent news conference, that also involved prisoner Brigadier-General Jemel Ahmed Hussein, Fahad claimed Iran had greatly improved its air defences since the 1986 offensive against the Fao peninsula to the south. The Iranians by the end of the month claimed to have downed another thirty-one Iraqi war planes.

In the meantime the Iraqi air force throughout January 1987 flew 200 raids in its unrelenting 'War of the Cities' against thirty-five Iranian towns. By the end of that month 7,786 Iranian civilians had been killed or wounded, which simply hardened Iran's determination to continue the conflict. Nor had Iran's air defences only improved over its oil facilities and the battlefield. On 14/15 February 1987 Iraq lost three more aircraft over Iran's southwestern towns. With seventy-two aircraft shot down, this led Saddam to call a two-week halt to the raids on civilian targets. These mounting losses were significant when considering between 1980 and 1984 Iraq had lost about 200 combat aircraft as well as seventy helicopters and several bombers.

Despite its success Iran's improved air defences were only short term, as they depended on adequate resupply plus the ability to man and operate the missiles and pay for them. By this stage in the war, the 'arms for oil' deals were common practice as both sides had run out of hard currency. Although Iran had succeeded in giving the Iraqi air force a bloody nose at the beginning of 1987, it had not solved its underlying lack of aircraft and aircrew.

Iraq, likewise, having suffered such a high attrition rate in aircraft over such a short period, lost a large number of very experienced pilots who were impossible to replace.

Iranian F-5 Tiger. (Khashayar Talebzadeh)

Iraqi 130mm field gun and antiaircraft guns. (U.S. DoD)

This 1984 Iraqi propaganda photo, taken at Salahedin PoW camp, near Tikrit, was in response to the visit by the International Red Cross who were viewing the state of Iranian prisoners. Those seen here are Iranian airmen.

Saddam had grossly miscalculated when it came to Iran's ability to defend its skies. Regardless of its significant numerical superiority, the Iraqi air force had proved unable to beat Iran into submission on its own.

Saddam's Hussein's strategic bombing campaign proved a failure. On a tactical level this suggested that the Iraqi air force would have been better employed in a combined operations role with the army. The latter could certainly have done with more help as it sought to beat off Iran's massed human-wave attacks.

At the same time the Iranians found it hard to hit back. Iran, with inferior resources, had to hold back the bulk of its operational aircraft and trained pilots for home defence, making it only possible to launch nuisance raids against Iraq. Fortunately, in July 1988, Iran finally agreed to a ceasefire, bringing the bitter battle for the skies to an end.

An Iranian M47 traversing the Hawizeh marshes. (Tom Cooper)

A captured Iraqi ZSU-57-2 self-propelled anti-aircraft gun. (Tom Cooper collection)

Destroyed Iraqi T-55s. (Tom Cooper collection)

Above: Iraqi T-72 in a
defensive hull-down position.
(Tom Cooper collection)

Right: Kurds inspecting the
wreckage of an Iraqi Mi-25.
(Tom Cooper collection)

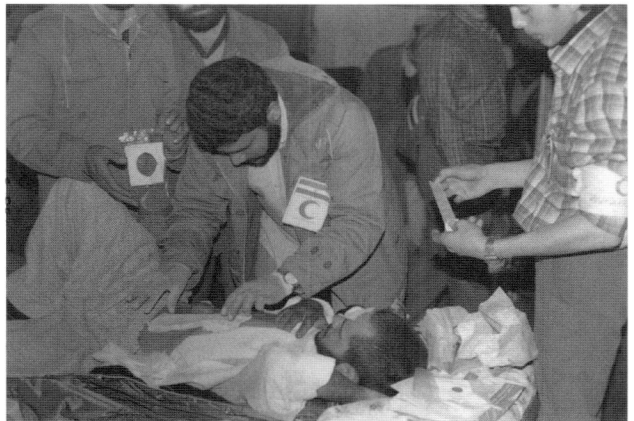

A field hospital of the Iranian
Red Crescent in action.
(Dabiri-e Vaziri)

9. NAVAL SKIRMISHES

When the Iran-Iraq War broke out Saddam's navy, numbering just 4,250 men, of whom 3,200 were conscripts, could put just five ex-Soviet large patrol craft, a dozen Osa fast-attack craft and another dozen P-6 fast-attack craft armed with torpedoes up against the Iranian navy. The latter, built up by the Shah, was 20,000 strong and equipped with an array of large surface vessels including three destroyers, four frigates, four corvettes, nine FAC(M)s and fourteen hovercraft.

Before the fall of the Shah, Iran had a number of vessels under construction abroad but after his demise they were impounded. For example, the supply vessel *Kharg* and her 200 crew were trapped in the UK. She was built for the Shah at the Swan Hunter yard on Tyneside and launched in 1977 as the *Princess Gholam Reza-Pahlavi*. Essentially she was a gun-armed support ship with a displacement of 10,900 tons capable of carrying three helicopters. The vessel had just completed trials when she became a victim of the December 1979 U.S. hostage crisis in Tehran in the wake of the Iranian Revolution. The *Kharg* was not delivered until the mid-1980s after much political wrangling.

In the late 1950s and early 1960s Moscow provided Baghdad with torpedo boats, smaller patrol craft and submarine chasers. Britain also supplied Iraq with patrol boats. Iraq's naval acquisitions paled into insignificance though, when compared to the vast array of larger warships that Iran was obtaining at the time, which included a destroyer and corvettes. What Iraq needed was a force multiplier in the shape of Soviet missile patrol boats, which were considered revolutionary when they appeared in the early 1950s. Torpedo boats were becoming increasingly vulnerable, as the North Vietnamese Navy (NVN) discovered in the early 1960s. Interestingly, while Moscow chose not to arm the NVN with missile boats, it looked upon Baghdad more favourably.

Initial Iraqi naval imports were followed by four Soviet Osa-I and three Osa-II missile patrol craft, each armed with four SSN-2 Styx ship-to-ship missile (SSM) launchers. This created an effective fledgling Iraqi navy based at Basra on the Shatt al-Arab and Umm Qasr. This development was a concern to both the Kuwaitis and Iranians as the Styx missile—while primarily an antishipping weapon with a 200-kilometre range—could be used to attack coastal targets.

During 1975–76 Iraq received five additional Soviet Osa-IIs. The Iraqis were so enamoured with Styx that they began to develop their own indigenous versions. As far as Saddam was concerned missile patrol boats were just the start of things. He had vastly more ambitious aspirations for his fledgling fleet; what he wanted was major surface combatants. His programme of major warship acquisition became apparent in 1979 when a contract was signed with Yugoslavia to supply a 1,850-ton training frigate which was delivered in the early 1980s. Throughout the late 1970s Saddam courted the major warship manufacturers, for he planned to acquire a navy that could take on Iran's.

Saddam revealed the scale of his accelerated expansion programme for the Iraqi navy in early 1980, when he ordered eleven ships, four Lupo class frigates (dubbed *Hittin* by the Iraqis), six Wadi class corvettes (*Assad* or *Hussa el Hussair*) and a Stromboli class (*Agnadeen*) support ship from Italy worth $1.5 billion. To equip these vessels Iraq also ordered A-109 and AB-212 anti-submarine warfare helicopters as well as Albatross, Aspide and Otomat-2 SSMs. Iraqi oil dollars ensured that Saddam could obtained the best that money could buy.

On 23 September 1980 Iraq 'officially' scrapped the 1975 Treaty after invading Iranian territory. Three days later the Iraqi newspaper *Al Thawra* photographed elements of the Iraqi navy, in the form of a patrol boat armed with heavy machine guns fore and aft, motoring down the Shatt al-Arab in support of the triumphant Iraqi army. The gunners' eyes were directed skyward for fear of the Iranian air force.

Iran immediately declared the border a war zone and closed the Shatt al-Arab estuary ordering all vessels to leave as quickly as possible. Iranian warships machine-gunned any vessels flying the Iraqi flag, which, in theory, was all of them. Over seventy ships, with an insurance value of $400 million, were stranded and found themselves caught in the cross-fire. The waterway itself was sown with mines. Iran quickly rendered the Iraqi ports of Basra and Umm Qasr inoperable in order to cut off Iraq's oil exports.

Much of the Iraqi navy and the state-backed commercial shipping company Iraqi Line found themselves trapped at Basra and Khor al-Zubair to the north of Umm Qasr. Reportedly nine commercial ships were trapped in the vicinity of the former and another nine in Umm Qasr. War-risk insurance rates for the head of the Gulf went through the roof and some areas were subject to underwriters' individual discretion (such as Iran's oil terminal at Kharg Island which regularly became a war zone). The Iranian port of Khorramshahr fell to the Iraqis on 24 October 1980 giving Baghdad control of the Shatt al-Arab until 22 May 1982 when the Iranians recaptured it.

During the war the Iraqi navy spent most of its time holed up in its bases. It took a very limited role in the 'Tanker War', conducted in the Gulf with gusto by either side's air forces, though Iraqi patrol boats were used to fend off Iranian naval commando attacks on Iraqi oil platforms. In the mid-1980s China supplied Baghdad with possibly over a hundred Hai Ying-1/2—the HY-1/2 was essentially a copy of the Soviet Styx, designated by the West the CSSC-3 Silkworm and Seersucker respectively—coastal defence missiles to arm Iraq's Osa-IIs and its B-6 bombers (Chinese version of the Soviet Tu-16). Some thirty Chinese C-601 antiship missiles were also provided. Egypt, a staunch Iraqi ally, may have provided additional HY-2s as well.

Remains of a commercial vessel sunk in the Gulf. (Lloyd's of London/The Salvage Association, Dubai)

Saddam's artillery included 122mm guns such as this. (U.S. DoD)

The unscrupulous Chinese then did business with Tehran and in the late 1980s reportedly sold Iran up to 200 C-801 (similar to the French MM38 Exocet) and HY-2 antiship missiles. North Korea also may have supplied Iran with HY-2s. Iranian opposition sources claimed that Tehran signed the $400-million contract in 1986 for Chinese Silkworm missiles, the first shipment allegedly arriving at the southern Iranian port of Bandar Abbas in March of that year. A Silkworm hit the U.S.-flagged tanker *Sea Isle City* in Kuwaiti waters on 16 October 1987. After American complaints China denied any sale of such missiles to Iran, claiming that they had been diverted from a third party or captured from Iraq.

Two of the finished Iraqi corvettes and the support ship left Italy bound for Umm Qasr via Alexandra, Egypt, in 1987. They were on a fool's errand. While tanks and combat aircraft poured into Iraq, from China, France and the Soviet Union via Kuwait and Jordan, there was no way for Saddam to get hold of his new warships without passage through the Iranian-dominated Strait of Hormuz.

Iran had deployed Silkworm missiles at the mouth of the Hormuz and the Shatt al-Arab. These new Iraqi ships could not enter the Gulf without coming under missile attack, or sail north without having to fight a running battle with Iran's air force, navy and the Islamic Revolutionary Guards Corps navy and air force, so they were forced to return to Italy where they remained in limbo. All but two of the corvettes were completed, but in the event none was ever delivered due to the war and the subsequent arms embargo implemented after the Gulf War.

Kuwait, fearing Iran's Islamic Revolution, gave its full support to Baghdad. The very facilities that Iraq had coveted for so long were placed at its disposal. Kuwait effectively became an Iraqi port, replacing Basra as the point of entry for military imports; the Iraqi air force was also permitted to over fly Kuwaiti territory. Kuwait soon began to regret this course of action and to consolidate its hold on Bubiyan built a bridge in 1983. Within two years of the Iraqi invasion Tehran had carried the war back into Iraq. Once the Iranians had captured the Iraqi town of Fao on the west bank of the Shatt al-Arab in February 1986, they were only a few kilometres from the Kuwaiti border. These events also effectively ended any ambitions Iraq might have had for using the ports of the Shatt al-Arab as anchorage for its new warships.

Tehran, knowing of Kuwait's complicity with Saddam, warned that any aid to Iraq, such as the leasing of Bubiyan, would be considered a hostile act. Kuwaiti tankers ferrying Iraqi oil that was funding Baghdad's war effort soon found themselves the subject of unwanted Iranian military attention. This led to U.S. intervention and an American showdown with the Iranian navy, forcing Tehran to finally accept a ceasefire with Baghdad.

By the time the war came to an end, on paper the Iraqi navy had five frigates and thirty-eight patrol and coastal combatants including four corvettes. However, the four *Hittin* frigates, four *Hussa el Hussair* corvettes and the *Agnadeen* support ship remained

Saddam's small navy included four Osa-I fast attack craft. (U.S. DoD)

stranded in Italy. As the remaining frigate, the *Khaldoum*, was a training vessel, this meant the Iraqi navy's teeth arm really only consisted of eight Osa and six P-6 fast attack craft, supported by eight mine-warfare vessels and six amphibious support boats.

After the ceasefire Iraq moved quickly to clear the ports of Umm Qasr and Khor al-Zubair, demanding that the seventy-five commercial ships trapped in the Shatt al-Arab be moved. Work commenced at al-Zubair with the removal of six vessels either under their own power or tow. The first vessel to leave was a Kuwaiti cargo ship which sailed for the Kuwaiti port of Shuwaikh. Dredging also commenced at the port to allow access for medium-sized bulk carriers.

10. THE OIL TANKER WAR

The Persian Gulf was the scene of a unique air war that witnessed sophisticated jet fighters trying to sink enormous unarmed civilian supertankers. Bordered by the rich Arab oil states, the Gulf is some 500 miles long and about 130 miles wide, with only one entranceway to the south via the sixty-mile-wide strategically important Strait of Hormuz. Through this passes much of the world's oil supplies (*see* map 10).

The Iraqi air force first bombed a vessel in the Gulf in May 1981. It then continually sent jets and helicopters to the Khor Musa area to prevent ships from taking cargo to the northern Iranian port of Bandar Khomeini. This heralded the start of the 'Tanker War' that rapidly spread south. Initially such attacks were limited to general cargo and bulk carriers, and only affected the protagonists, but in 1984 events occurred that ensured Saddam's air war involved the entire Gulf. Saddam, as part of his war to bring Iran to its knees, announced his intention to strangle Iranian oil exports by getting his air force to lay siege to the vital Kharg Island oil terminal that handled 85 percent of Iran's exports. This heralded systematic Iraqi attacks on huge supertankers of up to a quarter of a million tons.

Iraq leased five Dassault-Breguet Super Étendard strike aircraft in October 1983. (French Air Force)

Egypt supplied Iraq with Tu-16 bombers during the war. (Egyptian Air Force)

Under the command of Air Marshal Hamid Sha'aban, the Iraqi air force launched a steady stream of air attacks on Kharg and those ships plying their trade in the northern Gulf. In the forefront of this campaign was the Super Étendard strike fighter that had been designed for the French navy. It was in October 1983 that Saddam Hussein received, on special terms, five Étendards capable of carrying the feared AM39 Exocet antishipping missile that had made a name for itself during the Falklands War. These generous terms were apparently on a sale-or-return basis pending delivery of Exocet-compatible Mirage F1EQ-5s. The highly versatile Exocet is a particularly deadly weapon that can be fired from jets, helicopters, warships, submarines and shore batteries. Once launched, this sea-skimming five-metre-long missile travels at over 700mph to an effective range of 70 kilometres. Flying at just one kilometre above the surface, initial guidance is inertial until the radar cuts in allowing it to get within 6,000 metres of a target before detection. Therefore it is very hard to take countermeasures against. Iraq deployed both the ship- and air-launched versions.

The General Council of British Shipping warned its members that Saddam seemed to have a virtually unlimited supply of Exocets: between 1983 and 1987 the Iraqis are believed to have obtained some 638 of these from France. While only six Iraqi missile-carrying patrol craft were assessed to be at large in the Gulf, the greatest threat to shipping came from Saddam's Exocet-armed F1 Mirage jet fighters.

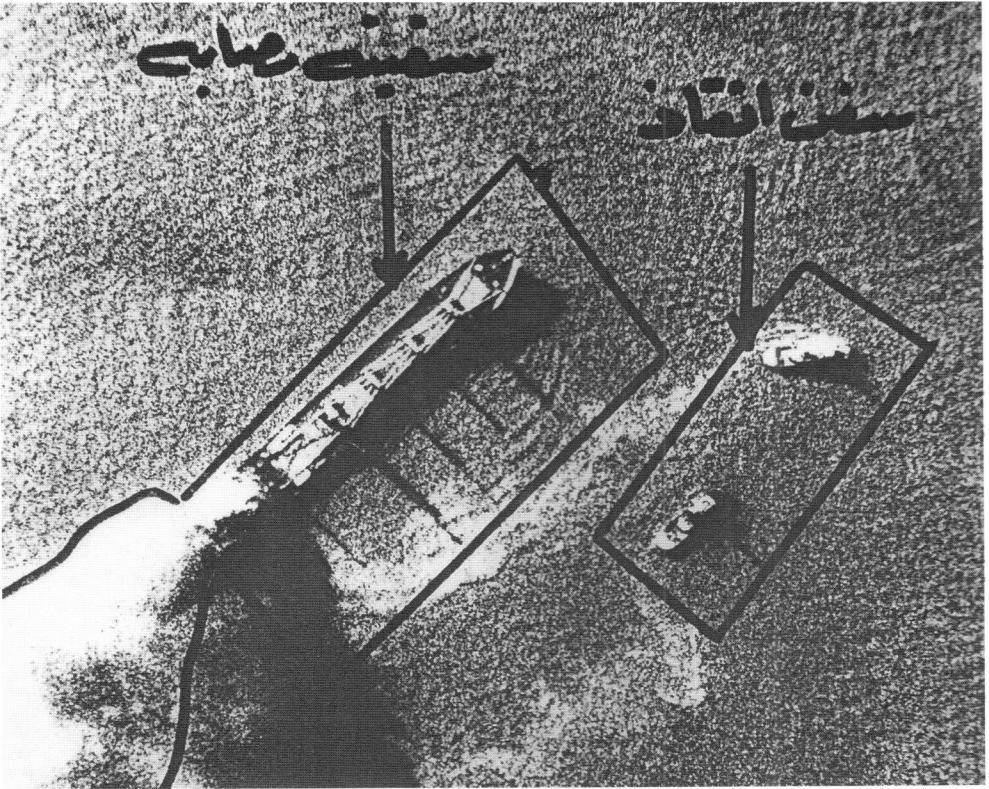

Iraqi intelligence photo showing a burning vessel in the Gulf in March 1984. (Iraqi News Agency)

Iranian marines prepare, February 1986. (Tom Cooper collection)

Egyptian support for Saddam also included Il-28 bombers. (Egyptian Air Force)

Between 25 February and 1 March 1984 Iraqi F1s hit seven ships in the Gulf. On 1 March they bombed a convoy approaching the Iranian port of Bandar Khomeini. A Turkish vessel was sunk and an Indian cargo vessel and the British bulk carrier *Charming* were damaged, resulting in a swift protest from the UK's Foreign Office. The attack though was simply a taste of things to come.

Iraqi naval chief of staff, Abelmohamed Abdallah, briefed reporters on the progress of the Iraqi air force attacks on 12 March 1984, triumphantly displaying photographs of burning and sinking vessels. It was fifteen days later that the Iraqi air force made its very first Super Étendard Exocet strikes. The last victim of the month was the Greek bulk carrier *Tapetos* hit on the 29th.

In the southern Gulf the Islamic Revolutionary Guard retaliated using small boats to attack tankers belonging to the neighbouring Gulf States providing financial support to Saddam's war effort. During the latter half of May 1984 Saddam called a halt to his air attacks, hoping that the show of strength would force Iranian leader Ayatollah Khomieni to the negotiating table, but he refused to talk. On 31 May 1984 Saddam threatened to destroy Kharg Island but Khomeini remained unmoved. In the meantime, thanks to the efforts of Iraqi pilots, the approaches to Kharg became known as 'bomb alley'. From 25 April to 3 June 1984 seven vessels were hit to the south of Kharg.

Iran's response was simple: rather than negotiate, it sought to drag in more countries which would force the international community to put pressure on Saddam to stop his land and air war against Iran. The Royal Saudi Air Force shot down an Iranian jet over Saudi territorial waters on 5 June 1984. Just five days later the first attack in the lower Gulf occurred when the 163,448-ton Kuwaiti tanker *Kazimah* was hit a hundred miles east of Qatar by a missile; two of its empty tanks were damaged but none of the crew was injured. Iran was held responsible. The Iranians said reprisals, mainly against Saudi and Kuwait ships, would only stop if Saddam lifted the exclusion zone he had instigated around Kharg Island.

A two-week UN-instigated lull ended on 24 June 1984 when the Iraqi air force launched its most daring raid on Kharg. Iraqi pilots penetrated the air defences, consisting of missiles and self-propelled antiaircraft guns, and pressed home their attacks on a Greek tanker and the offshore loading jetty. Although the jetty was put out of action for five days, Kharg's other jetty on the eastern side could still take large tankers. Three days later Saddam's Super Étendards struck the massive 260,000-ton, fully laden Liberian-registered *Tiburon*. Despite the Exocet being launched at extreme range, Iranian interceptors may have shot down one of Iraq's four remaining Étendards.

At the beginning of May 1984 when the 'Tanker War' commenced in earnest it seemed as if there would be another oil crisis. However, until Saddam resumed his aerial blockade of Kharg, output from the Gulf actually exceeded what is was before the war began. Market forces ensured that the world's tanker fleets remained prepared to brave 'bomb alley'. In addition a surplus of oil tankers meant they would fetch more in compensation if hit by an Iraqi or Iranian missile than if they were sold for scrap.

Saddam pressed on with his air raids, hitting about thirty ships between 1 January and 31 March 1985, the Iranians managing just seven. This meant that since March 1984 there had been up to sixty-five Iraqi airstrikes and twenty-five Iranian ones. Kharg Island continued to bear the brunt of Saddam's Gulf air war with the terminal enduring forty-five air raids between mid-August and early December 1985. To safeguard its customers Iran responded by creating a tanker shuttle service. Oil was ferried by Iranian chartered vessels 350 miles to the safer waters of Sirri Island where tankers could load up without being bombed.

The huge 170,053-ton Liberian tanker *Hawaii* was attacked by the Iraqis on 30 March 1986, making it the second largest vessel ever hit by either side. Also during this period the Norwegian *Berge King*, the *Zor* and the Panamanian *Stelios* were attacked by Iranian helicopters flying from the oil platforms known as Rostom Island about sixty-five miles from the Iranian coast. The Iranian military conducted fourteen such attacks in early 1986.

Previously, airstrikes centred on the shallows known as the Shah Allum Shoal close to Qatar's northern tip, had been carried out by the Iranian air force's American-supplied

The tanker *Hawaii* ablaze after an Iraqi airstrike in March 1986. (Lloyd's of London/The Salvage Association, Dubai)

The Iraqi Army Air Corps flew the Mi-24 helicopter gunship. (Author's collection)

F-4 Phantoms flying from Lavan Island just off the Iranian coast. However, Iranian jets were now being increasingly held back for air defence and ground support as the war deteriorated into a brutal slugging match. In a desperate bid to halt the escalating number of air attacks, the International Association of Independent Tanker Owners approached both governments but to no avail.

Instead Iran extended the area of its 'Tanker War' by establishing an airbase on Abu Musa Island sixty miles west of the strategic Strait of Hormuz. This placed Iranian aircraft and helicopters firmly within range of most shipping in the southern Gulf. At noon on 1 May 1986 British skipper David Lycett witnessed the Saudi tanker *Al Safaniya* hit in the crew's quarters by a missile-bearing helicopter believed to be Iranian. Lycett was organizing the fire-fighting when the helicopter returned, killing him and two Pakistani crew; seven others were wounded as the burning ship struggled to Abu Dhabi.

The Iraqi air force, growing in confidence, revisited Kharg on 29 March and 4 June 1986. Their next victim, the 155,887-ton *Medusa*, had the misfortune of being bombed for the third time in nine months just south of Kharg on 10 June 1986. The ship's boiler exploded, while the engine room, aft accommodation and the wheelhouse caught fire. By this date forty ships had been bombed during 1986 alone. The following day the Iraqis returned, catching the Maltese tanker *Lady Rose* south of Kharg; the ship suffered rudder damage and was left helplessly going round in circles.

Saddam's continued pressure on Kharg forced Iranian operations south, with the opening of the Valfjor oil terminal off Larak Island in the Strait of Hormuz. The move south from Sirri to Larak was to reduce insurance premiums for the tankers and make Iran's export crude oil more competitive. Iran's oil minister claimed it would make it possible to load tankers in complete safety.

Throughout July 1986 the Iraqi air force kept up the bombing of the eleven vessels of the Kharg shuttle service. At the end of July the 239,640-ton Greek supertanker *Polikon* was bombed three times off Kharg, until finally an Exocet punched a gaping hole in its portside. Two shuttle tankers were hit on 7 August 1986.

In the meantime the Iraqi air force had been planning a much longer-range mission. It launched its most audacious air attack on 12 August 1986. Skimming over the waves three Iraqi jets flew 550 miles to surprise twenty tankers at anchor off Sirri Island. The Iranians were caught completely off guard despite an earlier photoreconnaissance by four Iraqi planes on 24 June. The latter had resulted in the Iranians shifting some of their operations to Larak nearer the protection of the airbase at Bandar Abbas. Bad weather though had forced the Iranians to shift back to Sirri at the beginning of August, safe in the knowledge that Iraqi jets could not make the flight fully armed. However, the Iraqis, employing French laser-guided bombs, scattered twelve of the assembled ships, leaving three ablaze. Three missile were fired

Vessels in the Shatt al-Arab Waterway and the northern Gulf come under attack. (Lloyd's of London/ The Salvage Association, Dubai)

at the Liberian *Venture*, a mother ship used to store crude oil half a mile off Sirri: one missed, one hit the starboard hull near the waterline and the third bored into a cabin hatch. The 121,970-ton *Azarpad*, only 500 yards away, was engulfed in flames and sixteen crew killed.

For the Iranians and the international community this was an alarming development, as Sirri had previously been considered out of range of Saddam's jets. This attack seemed to imply in-flight refuelling or outside help. The death toll was also the highest for a single airstrike. The raid succeeded in forcing Iran to withdraw its storage fleet to Larak. This proved no safe haven from the marauding Iraqi air force. On 25 November 1986 Iraqi jets launched their longest raid yet, against Larak, a 1,560-mile round trip, hitting two tankers and a storage ship. Larak was again bombed on 28 January 1987. Then, on 17 May 1987, an Iraqi Mirage F1 'accidentally' fired two Exocet missiles into the U.S. warship U.S.S. *Stark*, killing thirty-seven crew and finally forcing greater U.S. and international intervention. By August that year foreign warships were patrolling the waters of the Gulf trying to prevent further air attacks on the world's shipping.

While Saddam temporarily refrained from attacks on Iran's oil facilities, Iran's response to international intervention in the Gulf was to lay mines and conduct a naval exercise, Operation *Martyrdom*, around Hormuz. Saddam recommended attacking Kharg

Burned-out wheelhouse of the *Polikon*, a victim of Iraqi missiles. This vessel was bombed three times off Kharg Island. (Lloyd's of London/The Salvage Association, Dubai)

Iranian 152mm howitzer in action. (Iranian Army)

Captured Iraqi T-55 and Rasit radar, Faw, 1986. (Tom Cooper collection)

on 30 August 1987 and both sides continued to bomb each other's oil facilities right until the end of the war.

The scale of the Gulf air war was massive. According to the insurers Lloyd's of London, between May 1981 and August 1987, at least 339 vessels were attacked or damaged by air or naval attack. Of these 115 ships were declared total losses due to the damage sustained. During 1987, by far the worst year, 178 ships were hit, with December being the worst with thirty-four strikes. In terms of human lives the real victims of the so-called Tanker War between 1984 and 1987 were 121 crew killed and an unknown number wounded. By the time the ceasefire came into effect, a total of 547 ships had been attacked of which 340 were tankers; 432 sailors had been killed.

However, the presence of the Exocet-armed Super Étendards did not prove as decisive as Saddam had hoped. His pilots were not persistent and failed to press home their attacks, launching their Exocets too far off; as a result, hits were well below the 60 percent achieved during the Falklands conflict. For example, around ninety-nine Exocets had been fired by August 1984 but only thirty-two actually struck targets. Crucially, the Exocet warhead was too small to sink an oil tanker. Under political pressure the Étendards were eventually returned to France in July 1985—the Iranians may have shot one down—and replaced by Mirage F1s. It was the latter that bore the brunt of the antishipping operations in the Gulf.

11. SWARMS OF INSECTS

Iraq took the decision in the mid-1970s to develop a full range of weapons of mass destruction (WMD), including chemical, biological, toxins, ballistic missiles and nuclear. However, the use of chemical and biological weapons was prohibited under international law, principally by the 1925 Geneva Protocol (to which Iraq and Iran were signatories) and the 1972 Biological Weapons Convention (Iraq signed the latter but did not ratify it, conveniently leaving it under no legal constraint).

The Geneva Protocol states simply, 'This prohibition shall be universally accepted as part of International Law, binding alike the conscience and practice of nations.' Fifty years after becoming a signatory Iraq, like a number of other rogue states, was to exhibit a conspicuous lack of conscience. In the face of what it deemed military necessity, over the next fifteen years Iraqi WMD efforts were considerable, encompassing a huge range of sites, some of which were vast. Saddam Hussein's accession to the Iraqi presidency in 1979, saw Baghdad accelerate its WMD programmes, sealing the fate of many Iranians and Kurds alike.

Iraq was to become the Middle East's biggest chemical weapons producer during the Iran-Iraq War. According to U.S. sources, Iraq's principal production facilities orbiting Baghdad, included al Fallujah (sixty-five kilometres to the west), Muthanna (seventy-three kilometres northwest), Samarra (a hundred kilometres northwest) and a research centre at Salman Pak (forty kilometres southwest). Additionally, the tried and tested Mustard gas (H agent) was also produced at Samawa (200 kilometres south of the capital) as well as nerve agents near the Jordanian border at Rutba. Most significantly, Iraq produced some 3.9 tonnes of the most devastating of them all, VX, at the Muthanna State Establishment, some of which was placed into Soviet-supplied Scud missile warheads.

Colonel-General Petrov, former head of the Soviet Union's chemical weapons, claimed Iraq had up to 4,000 tons of agents, mainly mustard gas, cyanide gas, Sarin (GB agent) and Tabun (GA agent). Iraq's initial stocks of Tabun allegedly came indirectly from the Soviet Union via Egypt, who had been supplied an unknown quantity of Second World War-vintage German Tabun in the 1960s (Soviet forces captured 12,000 tons and the Silesian factory in early 1945). This enabled the Iraqis to produce their own impure form of the gas. By the late 1980s it was estimated that Iraq could produce about 600 tonnes of nerve agent a year. During the early 1990s the UN identified stockpiles of not only the nerve agents GA and GB but also GF (similar to GB but less toxic).

Prior to the Iran-Iraq War, Iraq was also believed to have an operational biological weapons capability, producing, among other things, botulinum toxin. A delayed-action paralytic neurotoxin, it is about one thousand times more toxic than VX nerve agent. The Iraqis purchased equipment throughout Europe, ostensibly for their pharmaceutical industry, to produce human and animal vaccines. However, Iraq reportedly built biological plants, including al Hakam, capable of producing, anthrax, cholera and strains of typhoid and was looking at military applications for equine encephalitis and tularemia. The Kurdish Democratic Party (KDP) claimed bacteria was produced at Salman Pak, with related facilities at Akashat, Badoush, al Fallujah and Samarra.

In 1989, after the war had ended, Senator John McCain, a member of the American Senate Armed Forces Committee, stated Iraq was producing at least one lethal biological weapon and was engaged in research on microtoxins. Iraq found biological agents more difficult than chemical to weaponize and disseminate. According to the Iraqis the decision to develop biological wagons was taken in 1974, although Muthanna did not receive any bacterial strains until 1986. Work was conducted on anthrax and botulinum toxin and the following year the work was transferred to Salman Pak. Initial field trials were conducted in 1988. Many biological agents Iraq was working on were already prevalent in the region. For example, Iraq has about 100 to 200 reported cases of anthrax a year (which can affect its victim in three forms, cutaneous, pulmonary or gastrointestinal). Tularemia, plague, typhoid and cholera also naturally occur in the Middle East.

Iraq also worked successfully to increase the range of Soviet-supplied Scud missiles in order to hit Tehran and began work on the Badr-2000 (a 560-kilometre-range missile) based on Argentina's abandoned Condor-2. Other programmes included Canadian ballistics expert Dr Gerald Bull's 40-ton Supergun, which was designed to launch non-conventional warheads at Israel. Components for the latter were seized in the UK, Greece and Turkey. Bull himself was assassinated in Brussels in 1990, allegedly at the hands of Mossad, Israel's secret service.

Saddam's nuclear aspirations were considered such a threat that Israel bombed his Osirak reactor in 1981. It was assumed that this spelled the end of Iraq's nuclear programme, but this proved to be far from the case. Work continued at Tuwaitha (Baghdad's Nuclear Research Centre) and in 1982 work began on uranium-enrichment techniques. Baghdad's weapons programme was publicized in 1990 after dummy nuclear triggers destined for Baghdad were seized at Heathrow airport.

By the mid-1980s Saddam was struggling to contain Iran's vigorous counteroffensives and was looking to deploy a force multiplier which could offset the Iranians' superior manpower. Between May 1981 and March 1984 his forces resorted to chemical weapons forty-nine times, killing 1,200 and injuring 5,000. This was just a taste of things to come.

The Iranians, hoping to deliver a decisive knockout blow by severing the Basra–Baghdad highway, through the seizure of Basra and Qurna, launched three offensives in 1984. These would also drive a wedge between the Iraqi 3rd and 4th corps. The first offensive attempting to cut the highway between Amara and Kut was brought to a halt. However, elements of the waterborne offensive in the southern Iraqi marshes captured three floating villages, while others occupied the two important Majnoon Island oil facilities. Alarmingly for Saddam, the Iranians also reached the outskirts of Qurna. Two of Iraq's most important cities were in danger of being cut off, a potential disaster for Iraqi civilian and military morale. The Iraqi high command, perhaps panicking, decided to deploy mustard gas and possibly nerve agents.

Iraqi shells and rockets began to pour onto Iranian positions just like any other day in late February 1984, only on this occasion there was an overpowering odour of garlic. Slowly Iranian soldiers began to choke to death and others fled back through their lines bearing terrible burns. The Iraqis counterattacked on at least six occasions using chemical weapons, beating back the Iranians at Qurna, but failing to regain the Majnoon. U.S. intelligence sources suspected the use of mustard gas. Its symptoms are difficult to deny: the liquid destroys skin tissue, causing severe blistering, while its vapour attacks the eyes, respiratory track and moist areas of the body.

Evidence that Saddam was also using nerve agents emerged in the second week of March 1984. In the Gzaiel sector forty-five kilometres north of Basra, Iranian dead, many of them without any marks, were found carrying self-injecting ampoules of atropine sulphate, a drug used as an antidote to nerve-gas poisoning. Up until this point Iran was alleging Iraqi chemical weapons had killed 12,000 of its troops and injured 5,000. Iranian forces now had to permanently carry gasmasks.

Iraq made itself perfectly clear where it stood on the issue of chemical weapons. In mid-March 1984 Iraqi Major-General Maher Abd Rashid stated, 'If you give me a pesticide to throw at these swarms of insects ... then I'd use it.' A UN investigative team visited Iran and concluded mustard gas and perhaps Tabun had been used, but bizarrely did not directly accuse Iraq of being the culprit.

From 12 March 1985 the Iraqis used chemical weapons over a four-week period to drive off Iran's Operation *Badr*. According to Iranian reports 4,600 troops were killed or wounded in thirty-four separate chemical attacks. Reports from Tehran of further attacks continued during April, May and November 1985. The Iranians claimed there were forty-six air, artillery and mortar attacks using nerve, blood, blister and choking gases.

Despite a mounting chorus of disapproval within the UN, the Iraqis resolutely denied all allegations and the Security Council avoided outright condemnation. Evidence though consistently pointed to the Iraqis using mustard gas, Lewisite (another blister agent), Tabun and possibly hydrogen cyanide (a lethal, non-persistent blood agent).

Saddam's use of these weapons peaked during the second week of February 1986, when around 10 percent of the Iranian forces attacking Fao became chemical casualties. Appallingly, some 2,000 received mustard gas burns on 13 February alone. Iranian sources

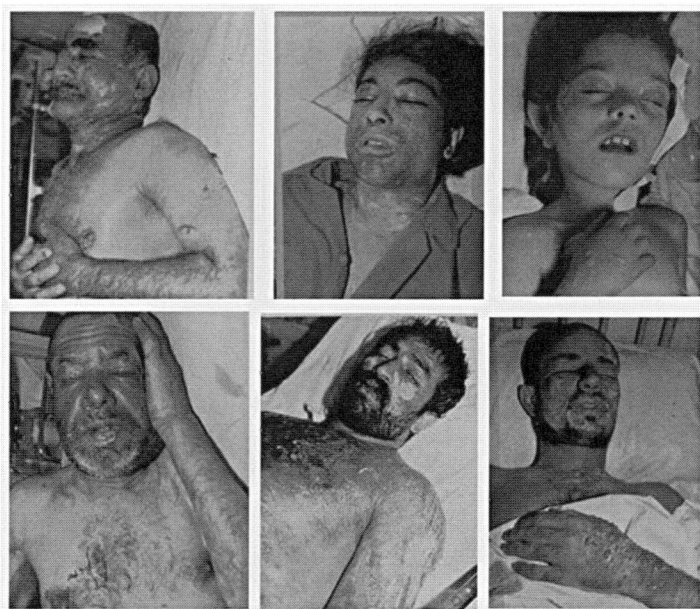

Kurdish victims of
Iraqi mustard-gas
attacks on Sardasht,
West Azerbaijan
Province, Iran,
28 June 1987.

claimed 8,500 Iranians had fallen victim to the renewed Iraqi use of chemical weapons. The British government conservatively estimated by this stage in the war that there had been 10,000 Iranian chemical weapon casualties. Reports confirmed Saddam's flagrant violation of the Geneva Protocol. According to the UN, in March 1986, a team, after examining over 700 Iranian chemical weapon casualties in Ahwaz and Tehran, concluded that Iraq had been using mustard and nerve gases. The assessment noted, 'It is our impression that the use of CW in 1986 appears to be more extensive than in 1984.' Iraq reportedly employed both nitrogen mustard and nerve gas. Although the report condemned Iraq by name for the first time, the Security Council simply registered its disapproval. Saddam was not deterred in the least.

Saddam resorted to such weapons because it helped break up Iran's massed infantry attacks, it was easy to produce in adapted petroleum plants and it suited the climate. In cold weather mustard gas is a yellowish fluid that sticks, in a hot climate it vaporizes causing even greater respiratory damage. Cheaper than conventional weaponry, as a force multiplier it worked. The scale of the casualties escalated from eleven in 1981 to 13,000 a year in 1987 and 1988. Iran claims that in 242 attacks between January 1981 and March 1988 it lost 44,000 troops to Iraqi chemical weapons. After the war Tehran estimated that 100,000 Iranian soldiers and civilians had been exposed to Saddam's chemical arsenal.

12. JETS OVER HALABJA

At the outbreak of war the Iraqi Kurdish Peshmerga grasped the opportunity to reassert their rights and renewed the guerrilla struggle against the Iraqi armed forces. Iranian leader Ayatollah Khomeini also restored Tehran's military support. For the time being Saddam Hussein had his hands full with his invasion of Iran, but he was just biding his time: he would not tolerate the constant threat to the northern flank of his armies.

Iran, allegedly helped by the KDP, moved against Iranian Kurdish forces operating out of Iraq, in July 1983, capturing Hajj Omran. Baghdad's response was to round up 8,000 Kurds who were never heard of again. This was a taste of things to come. The following year the Iranians reportedly threw 250,000 troops against 15,000 Iranian Kurdish guerrillas. By late 1983 the PUK allegedly came to a truce with Baghdad, but after two years it had come to nothing. While the Kurdish forces were not strong enough to topple the Iraqi government, by 1985 the KDP was holding down an Iraqi division in the Zakho area (the Iraqi, Turkish and Syrian border zone). Significantly the following year the feuding KDP and PUK agreed to work together.

With the Iraqi army distracted by Iranian efforts in the south of the country, in early 1987 PUK guerrillas began to return to their strongholds overlooking Sulaymaniyah and the road linking it with the oil city of Kirkuk. Iran, pushing twenty kilometres to Rayat on the Rowanduz road, weakened Iraq's hold on the area. Over the end of April and early May 1987 the guerrillas, aided by deserting Kurdish government militiamen, captured seven towns (up to 4,000 *Jash* or Kurdish government troops were reported to have come over to the KDP). In early September 1987 the Iraqis counterattacked with four divisions totalling 30,000 regular troops and 30,000 militia. This heralded the infamous al-Anfal campaign that was to kill an estimated 100,000 to 180,000 Kurds.

Tragically, the writing was on the wall for Iraq's Kurds, but no one spotted the warning signs until it was too late. After Iran's success in Iraqi Kurdistan in October 1983, Baghdad officials began to talk threateningly of a 'new and secret weapon'. In January 1988 KDP forces captured documents at Deralok relating to Iraqi chemical weapons, one of which was a letter from Iraqi General Deah Abdul Wahhab Izzat based at Arbil (Erbil). Dated 3 August 1986 it was headed 'Control over distribution of biological and chemical materials' and called for a half-yearly stocktake of all such weapons held by Iraqi units in the area. Clearly they were in place; it was just a matter of when and where would Saddam choose to deploy them.

In the spring of 1988 the Iraqis launched a major offensive out of Arbil designed to cut the guerrillas' vital Iranian supply routes. Seven Iraqi divisions east of Lake Dukan attempted to capture the PUK's HQ at Yakhsamar. It was now that the Kurds began to claim that Iraqi forces were using blister and nerve agents. Between April 1987 and August 1988 Kurds claimed the Iraqi air force used chemical weapons against their villages at least 200 times. These though were all on a small scale and were nothing compared to the horror that was about to be unleashed upon the Kurdish mountains.

After the failure of Tehran's southern offensive against Basra in 1987, Iranian efforts once again gravitated toward the northern Kurdish front, with an attempt to capture the hydroelectric plant on Lake Darbanikha that supplied Baghdad. The PUK captured nine towns including Khormal and Halabja but lacking heavy weapons were unable to hold them. The Iraqi army promptly reoccupied Halabja, a town of 70,000 some twenty-two kilometres from the Iranian border. Iran, having mustered its forces, launched Operation *Zafar 7* near Khormal and Operation *Bait al-Muqaddas 3* north of Sulaymaniyah on 13 March 1988, employing several divisions. Shortly after, along with their Kurdish allies, they launched *Val Fajr 10*.

In just two days of fighting the Iranians claimed to have killed or wounded 5,500 Iraqi troops and captured Khormal, followed by Halabja and much of the lake on 16/17 March 1988. Cut off and surrounded by up to 20,000 Iranian troops, Iraqi General Ali Hussein Al-Gowi and his 1,5000-strong Halabja garrison laid down their arms without firing a shot. Most of the occupying Iranian forces camped outside the town and up to half the population fled for fear of reprisals. The PUK also claimed credit for taking Halabja, saying the Iranians had only captured Khormal. According to KDP commanders, it was their men, who for the loss of just seven guerrillas, seized a key bridge cutting off the Halabja area and then ambushed Iraqi reinforcements. It mattered little: all Saddam Hussein cared about was that the town had fallen into his enemies' hands.

Saddam swiftly took the fateful decision to make an example of the Kurds and to unleash chemical weapons en masse against a civilian target. In charge of this operation was his cousin, General Ali Hassan al-Majid, whose actions were to gain him the titles 'Chemical Ali' and 'Butcher of Kurdistan'. While it is generally assessed that the Iraqis never used VX against the Iranians, it is possible that they now added it to their cocktail of cyanide and mustard gas destined for Halabja. The Iraqi air force launched its biggest chemical attack of the war on 16 March 1988. From 11.15 a.m. to just after 2 p.m. the Iraqis dropped conventional cluster bombs to force the population to flee, then the explosions became more muffled. Tehran claims that cyanide was dropped by the Iraqis in a large area of central Halabja, while mustard and nerve gas were used on the suburbs.

When the dust settled the scale of the carnage was shocking. Iraqi pilots, normally fearful of Iranian air defences, tended to fly too high when dropping chemical bombs, resulting in the agent being spread over too wide an area to be effective, with it some-times blowing back over their own army. On this occasion they seemed to have achieved a high degree of accuracy: thousands lay dead in the dirt streets or strewn in their homes and courtyards. The killing was indiscriminate. Most victims appeared to have suffocated in seconds: a mother lay cradling her baby, a family of three together, a father trying to protect his child from the white clouds of vapour. According to the Iranians, the cyanide dropped by the Iraqis in 100-litre containers vaporized immediately on impact. None of the dead bore external injuries.

Up to half the town's remaining population were casualties, suffering up to 5,000 dead and a further 8,000 injured by the choking fumes (the KDP put the final death toll at 12,000). Fearing the Iraqis might attack again and with pockets of gas still in the cellars, burials were not completed until the end of the month. The swiftness of the massacre clearly indicated something fast-acting that affected the circulation, such as a nerve agent (Sarin or Tabun).

Reportedly a combination of cyanide, nerve gas and mustard gas was used. Indeed sub-sequent soil samples proved that the Iraqis had used at least mustard and nerve agents. Three days later, on 19 March 1988, the PUK HQ at Yakhsamar was reported to have fallen.

If the retreating Peshmerga thought the attack on Halabja was an isolated punishment for collaborating with Iran, they were wrong. The Iraqi air force resumed operations just ten days after the gassing of Halabja. On March 26 and 27 Iraqi jets dropped chemical bombs near the Kurdish city of Karadagh, killing sixty-four and injuring two hundred and ten. Iranian troops also suffered in these attacks, many were injured when Iraqi jets dropped chemical bombs in an attempt to drive off an offensive around Panjwin, a Kurdish town 280 kilometres northeast of Baghdad, on 12 April 1988.

Unfortunately for the Kurds these were just the opening shots in a sustained chemical weapons offensive against them, which accelerated once an Iran–Iraq ceasefire came into effect. Iran agreed to stop supporting the KDP on condition Iraq stop backing Iranian Kurds and Iranian mujahedeen forces. With a ceasefire date agreed for August, Iranian forces withdrew from the Halabja area on 12 July 1988. Baghdad was now able to turn its battle-hardened 7th Corps and Republican Guard Corps on the Kurds, the offensive open-ing a week later. By August 1,900 civilians had been killed and 5,000 injured.

While Halabja attracted the attention of the world's media, another massacre five months later went largely unnoticed. On 28 August 1988, in a repeat performance, the Iraqi air force attacked Bassay Gorge, thirty kilometres south of the Turkish border. One of the Kurdish guerrillas watching helplessly from the hillsides observed: 'There must have been 3,000 bodies and thousands of animals, all dead. The dead had film over their eyes and out of their noses and from the sides of their mouth there was a horrible slime coming out. The skin was peeling and bubbling.' Thousands were also feared dead in

This massacre of Iranian civilians by Iraqi troops took place early in the war, c. 1981. (Saeed Jabozorgy)

Sheikhan and KDP sources claimed that another 1,500 Kurds, including women and children, were gassed during August 1988.

A Peshmerga guerrilla and former student recalled with dismay: 'We did not imagine it could come on such a horrific scale. It was more wide-spread and brutal than Halabja. This is a war of extermination ...' The Peshmerga, who had few if any gasmasks, claimed the Iraqis used aircraft, including crop sprayers, artillery, and rocket launchers to deliver the chemicals. The attacks continued well into October 1988 in Kirkuk province, where some 2,000 Peshmerga were still operating.

Kurdish opposition sources also claimed biological weapons were deployed by the Iraqi air force, leading to outbreaks of cholera and typhoid. Kurds stated that biological weapons were used on Sulaymaniyah in September 1988 when allegedly typhoid bombs were dropped by the Iraqi air force. Kurds in the Mardin refugee camp inside Turkey in July 1990 claimed the Iraqis had poisoned their bread supplies. Claiborne Pell, chairman of the U.S. Senate Foreign Relations Committee, despatched a two-man team to Turkey in 1988 to investigate. They concluded that Baghdad was deliberately using chemical weapons as part of an effort to depopulate Kurdistan, noting, 'The end result of this policy will be the destruction of the Kurdish identity, Kurdish culture, and a way of life that has endured for centuries.' It was an accurate summation.

13. FOUGHT TO A STANDSTILL

Iran's acceptance of UN Resolution 598 and the ceasefire on 20 August 1988 can largely be seen as the result of deputy supreme commander and speaker of the parliament Akbar Hashemi Rafsanjani's pragmatic assessment of Iran's crippled armed forces. Recruitment was down, morale of the fanatical Revolutionary Guard Corps and the army had plummeted, supply sources were ad hoc and terrible casualties had sapped the political will. This led the Iranian leadership to the conclusion that it was futile to continue the struggle against Saddam who had accepted the resolution in July 1987.

While numerous factors swayed Tehran's agreement to a ceasefire, it is generally agreed that Iran's massive losses for little military gain was the deciding one. In particular, the bloody campaign fought in the killing grounds to the east and northeast of Basra in 1987, which cost the Iranians up to 100,000 casualties, is seen as the decisive battle that finally broke the back of the Iranian armed forces. Analysis of the statistics of all the major battles shows that both sides endured the most appalling losses. Despite a tendency to exaggerate each other's losses, Iran consistently suffered higher casualties.

At the beginning of the war Iran's total forces numbered some 240,000—army 150,000, air force 70,000 and navy 20,000—plus reserves of 400,000. Thanks to the turmoil of the revolution, desertion and purges, the army's strength had fallen by about 60 percent, the air force by 20 percent and the gendarmeries by 75 percent. Remarkably, by 1982, Iran's forces had made a rapid recovery with the population mobilized for war on a massive scale.

Exact figures for the losses incurred during the opening phase of the war in 1980/1 are understandably unclear, but as Iran began to go over to the counterattack the fighting became increasingly intense. In the space of two months between the end of September 1981 and November 1981 the Iranians reportedly inflicted 3,500 casualties on the Iraqis. On 22 March 1982 Operation *Fath Ul-Mobin*, in which 100,000 Iranian troops were committed against 70,000 Iraqis west of Dezful and Shush, drove the Iraqis back almost to the border. The Iraqi army seems to have been taken by surprise suffering 8,000 killed, 12,000 wounded and 13,000 to 20,000 captured for the loss of 5,000 Iranians.

When the brutal siege of Khorramshahr was lifted by Operation *Bail Ul-Moqaddas*, launched on 24 May 1982, the vengeful Iranians inflicted a further 16,000 Iraqi casualties and took 17,500 prisoners. Losses suffered by both sides in and around the city are assessed to have totalled 20,000, with some 30,000 Iraqis being captured. This major defeat forced the Iraqi army to redeploy to the border, leaving behind 50,000 dead and 50,000 PoWs.

It was on 14 July 1982 that Iran took the fateful decision to take the war into Iraq with Operation *Ramadan* launched toward Basra. In the face of determined Iraqi defences, with two attempts Iran failed to take the city or cut the Baghdad highway, sustaining up to 100,000 casualties in the process. The Iraqis, being on the defensive, only suffered 7,000 killed and wounded with just 1,400 men captured. Operation *Muslim Ibn Aquil*, conducted from 1 to 10 October 1982, had a similar outcome. The Iranians achieved greater success in driving the Iraqis out of Iranian territory west of Dezful in Operation *Muharram*, between 1 and 11 November 1982, inflicting 6,200 Iraqi casualties and capturing a further 3,500.

Things did not go well for Saddam's army the following year when it suffered a series of defeats. They lost 8,500 men in April 1983 to Iran's Operation *Val Fajr 1* on the southern front, 10,500 in July south of Mehran to *Val Fajr 3* and 9,500 on the Kurdish front to *Val Fajr 4*. These victories though came at a cost, yet the ayatollahs seemed to care little for human life. For example, on 6 February 1983, they threw 200,000 troops into an offensive southeast of Baghdad, losing 6,000 men in a single day. By the end of the year the Iranians had suffered 120,000 dead and 30,000 PoWs.

The bloodletting was clearly unrelenting. The ayatollahs were determined to punish Saddam for his aggression and kept up the pressure. Between September 1981 and January 1984 the Iranians launched a total of thirteen major offensives, of which roughly five were at corps and four at divisional strength. During these attacks Iran claimed to have inflicted a total loss on the Iraqis of some 114,111 (71,954 killed and 42,157 PoWs); this roughly tallies with other independent estimates of around 80,000 dead and 150,000 wounded.

In stark contrast by March 1984 a senior officer in the Iranian Army Medical Corps claimed his country had lost a staggering 400,000 men. The previous year, on 1 May 1983, Iraq stated it had killed 291,984 Iranians in war related action, and by 1984 even conservative estimates were 170,000 Iranian dead and twice that wounded. Iran was thought to be holding about 50,000 Iraqi PoWs while Iraq only had 7,300, the latter possibly indicating a measure of Iranian fanaticism.

Despite these appalling losses, the ayatollahs massed 500,000 troops and launched three offensives over February and March 1984 north of Basra. During the second attack conducted on 22 February the Iranians lost 20,000 men and the Iraqis 7,000. At the height of this brutal battle where over half a million troops were involved, by its climax the Iraqi army claimed to have slaughtered 30,000 Iranian soldiers, including 2,000, most of whom were gassed, in the battle of Gzaeil. The Iranians claimed 12,000 Iraqi fatalities.

U.S. intelligence indicated the widespread use of mustard gas by this stage. Between May 1981 and March 1984 the Iraqis were reported to have used chemical bombs on forty-nine occasions, killing 1,200 Iranians and injuring a further 5,000. In the battles fought during February and March 1984 another 3,000 soldiers and civilians were gassed.

The MT-LB was used by the Iraqis as an armoured personnel carrier and artillery tractor. (U.S. DoD)

Both sides claimed victory in the Iran-Iraq War, but in reality fought each other to a bloody standstill. (via Author)

Both sides reportedly suffered combined losses of 40,000 men on 18 October 1984 when Iran launched an offensive overlooking the Tigris plain. After forcing the Iraqis back over the border, Iraq counterattacked two days later destroying Iranian gains.

The bloodletting had been such that the following year Iran was only able to muster 50,000 men for the offensive Operation *Badr* conducted on 11 March 1985. Caught by a well-timed Iraqi counterattack, 15,000 Iranians were killed in the marshes northwest of Basra. Iraqi casualties were also reportedly heavy, amounting to some 10,000.

Ironically, Iran's first real strategic success occurred with surprisingly light losses. In February 1986, in Operation *Val Fajr 8* involving up to 100,000 troops, the Iranians successfully captured the Fao peninsula at a cost of 2,500 men, while inflicting 4,000 casualties on the Iraqis and capturing 1,500. This provided a southern springboard against Basra. Holding on to it though did not warrant the loss of a further 20,000 men during February and March 1986 when the Iraqis counterattacked, suffering about 6,000 casualties, although the Iranians put the figure at double this.

Perhaps, understandably, by the spring of 1987 Iranian zeal for waging war was waning. Tellingly, only 12 percent of the fanatical Revolutionary Guards were volunteers. None of the army's armoured units was more than 17 percent of normal strength and none of the artillery units was fully operational.

The battles that finally broke the Iranian armed forces were Operation *Karbala 5* that began on 9 January 1987 and *Karbala 8*, launched on 6 April 1987 and involving 350,000 Iranian troops. By 22 February the Iranians had pushed to within twelve miles of Basra and killed or wounded 33,000 Iraqis at a cost of 90,000 men. When the offensive ground to a halt on 1 April just six miles from Basra the Iranians had suffered 100,000 casualties. Conservative estimates place it at 40,000 but this is probably the figure for the dead. The Iraqis who fought a well-executed defensive battle suffered up to 45,000 killed and wounded.

The continual failure of these massive Iranian military operations meant that by 1988 Iran was unable to mark the tenth anniversary of the revolution with its customary annual spring offensive in the south. This was due to a shortage of troops, especially officers and non-commissioned officers, as well as weapons. Also recruitment was reportedly down by 50 percent, raising only 100,000 men instead of the 200,000 target.

Instead, Iranian efforts were shifted to the Kurdish front. In February 1988 the Iraqis launched an offensive against the Kurds. The Iranians with their Kurdish allies in March took Khormal and Halabja along with some 2,000 prisoners and inflicting 7,000 casualties on the Iraqis in the fighting. By 11 April the Iranians claimed to have inflicted another 5,000 casualties and taken 700 PoWs. To the south Saddam seized the initiative liberating the Fao peninsula with Operation *Ramadan Mubarak* in April 1988. In the process he overcame the 30,000-strong Iranian garrison—although it was rumoured to be only 5,000–7,000—and taking just 200 prisoners.

Iraqi Chinese-built Type 69 tank. The Chinese cynically sold weapons to both sides. (U.S. DoD)

At the start of the Iran-Iraq War the Iraqis had a dozen missile-armed patrol boats—such as the Osa-II. (U DoD)

Between January 1984 and April 1988 Iran launched fourteen major operations with very limited results. On 25 May 1988 the Iraqis successfully drove the Iranians out of the Shalamcheh sector fifteen miles east of Basra. In an effort to boost falling morale the Iranians launched a counteroffensive on 13 June, claiming to have inflicted 12,000 to 16,500 casualties and taken 2,200 PoWs. This victory was short-lived, as in June 1988 they lost 6,000 killed and 1,500 captured when the Iraqi-backed anti-Khomeini National Liberation Army (NLA) took Mehran.

Then, on 25 June, the Iraqis retook the Majnoon oilfields destroying a force of about 10,000, capturing 2,000 PoWs; a chemical attack killed 60 Iranians and injured 4,000 near Ahwaz. A further 20,000 Iranians were killed and wounded and 6,000 captured on 19 July when the Iraqis took Dehloran nineteen miles inside Iran prior to securing the Zubeidat border area. This meant the Iranians were driven out of all their Iraqi footholds. The Iraqis, now in a firm negotiating position, offered peace on 19 July 1988; the Iranians accepted the UN Resolution the following day.

Determined to strengthen his hand, Saddam's forces pushed on toward Ahwaz on 22 July, taking 8,635 PoWs and killing or wounding a further 4,000. The Iranians claimed to have driven the Iraqis back, inflicting 4,000 casualties, followed by a further 1,500 three days later despite the Iraqis having withdrawn. The Iraqis also lost 3,000 casualties in securing the Qasr-e-Shirin–Khosrai sector after pushing twelve miles into Iran. The NLA claimed an exaggerated 40,000 casualties between 25 and 28 July; Iran claimed to have killed 4,500 of them while driving them off.

By the end of July 1988, in just six days Iraq claimed to have taken 12,207 PoWs, a vital bargaining chip. According to figures released by the International Committee of the Red Cross, Iran had 49,285 Iraqi prisoners, while Iraq had only 12,747 Iranians. This latter figure might have been due to prisoners being released to fight with the NLA. However, diplomats in Baghdad put the PoW figures at 70,000 Iraqis and up to 35,000 Iranians. Other sources quoted 50,000 Iraqi prisoners and 35,000 Iranians. Iran put its number of missing in action at 30,000 while Iraq had some 20,000 unaccounted for. In 1987 some 7,000 Iraqi prisoners were removed from the Iranian register for reasons that are unclear. Furthermore, there were some 20,000 foreign prisoners of war, mainly Egyptians and Sudanese, but also Jordanians, Moroccans, Palestinians and Tunisians. The vast majority of them fought for Iraq, though Iran attracted numbers of fundamentalist Islamic foreign fighters.

In terms of casualties the Iran-Iraq War was the third-largest post-Second World War conflict after Korea and Vietnam. Total Iranian losses probably amounted to at least a million, with lower estimates of 750,000 to 900,000. At least 40,000-plus casualties were sustained on the Iranian home front. In January 1987, in Saddam's 'War of the Cities' the Iranians suffered 7,786 casualties. Saddam's missile blitz between 1 March and 12 April 1988 inflicted a further 10,200 casualties. It is quite possible that Iran's losses were in excess of 1.5 million.

Iraqi casualties are in the region of at least 400,000 to 500,000, although the official death toll was only acknowledged as 160,000. It is ultimately impossible to be precise about either side's losses especially when they were so obscured by propaganda.

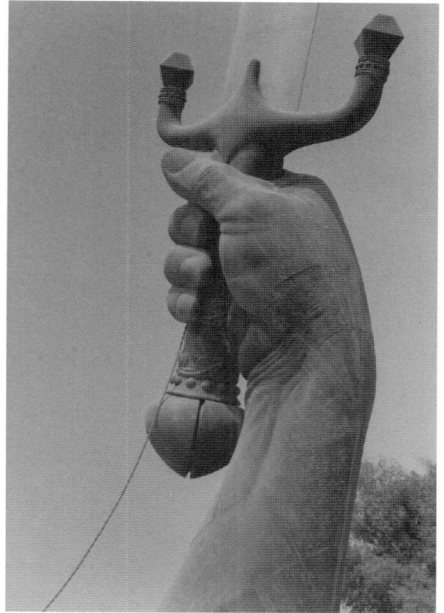

Right: One of the hands forming Baghdad's triumphal arch—Saddam claimed a hollow victory over Iran. (Author's Collection)

Below: The 2S1 122mm self-propelled gun employed by the Iraqi army. (U.S. DoD)

Islamic Revolutionary Guards, Operation *Badr*, March 1985. (Tom Cooper collection)

By 1989 Iran's total armed forces numbered 604,500. The army had some 305,000 troops, equipped with 1,000 tanks, 410 armoured personnel carriers and 1,000 antiaircraft guns. It was organized with three army HQs, four mechanized divisions, six infantry divisions, one Special Forces division, one airborne brigade and twelve surface-to-air missile battalions. The Revolutionary Guards who had borne the brunt of the war numbered 250,000 with the *Basij* militia numbering anything between 150,000 and 250,000.

The Iranian navy was down to 14,500 personnel including the naval air elements and marines, equipped with three destroyers, five frigates, thirty-four patrol craft and fourteen armed helicopters. The air force was down to half strength at 35,000 airmen with just fifty combat aircraft. The gendarmerie numbered about 45,000 with 2.5 million Home Guard.

Saddam's regular forces by contrast were much larger, at one million, with an army of 955,000, air force of 40,000 and navy of 5,000. Other sources though put the number of Iranians still under arms much higher at 2.5 million of which two million were regulars, with another one million available for mobilization, though this does seem unreasonably high after all Iran's losses.

Iranian population growth was such that it was unable to keep pace with Iran's terrible battlefield losses. Iran still had at this stage 500,000 men eligible for military service annually, while Iraq could call on just over 170,000. In total Iran had a manpower pool of seven million while Iraq could call on only two million. Although the ayatollahs could have continued their bloody war of attrition, after eight years it appeared that Iran had been finally fought to a standstill.

14. THE AFTERMATH

The aftermath of the Iran-Iraq War saw growing unrest in both countries. The ceasefire did not shield either Iran's or Iraq's armed forces from further upheaval. Saddam swiftly redeployed his battered ground forces in a major effort to crush Kurdish separatist aspirations once and for all. Also there were constant accusations of border violations even though hostilities had officially ceased. Having built up such vastly powerful armed forces, both government' sought to ensure their continued political dominance. This led to a number of publicized coup attempts.

At the beginning of February 1989 Saddam Hussein reportedly thwarted a coup involving those forces stationed in the north (1st Special Corps east of Mosul, 2nd Corps around Sulaymaniyah and 5th Corps along the Turkish border). It was also rumoured that officers from the elite and politically reliable Iraqi Republican Guard were involved. Initial reports stated between December 1988 and February 1989 some 200 officers and civilians were executed as traitors. Other more conservative estimates of fifty arrested, retired or executed with only around eight generals or colonels actually shot are probably more accurate. Whether this plot was very widespread or even actually existed is not entirely clear. It may be that Saddam was simply purging those officers he felt were untrustworthy or posed a potential threat. Certainly, during the course of the war a number of nearly successfully assassination attempts were made against him. He also viewed some of Iraq's war heroes as potential opposition figures who could not be tolerated.

One such veteran was the highly respected General Maher Abd al-Rashid, commander of the Iraqi 3rd Corps on the bloody southern front. He was placed under house arrest after protesting about the unequal distribution of medals to the Republican Guard at the end of 1988. Saddam's brother-in-law, General Adnan Khairallah, was relieved at the beginning of March 1989 in part of a deliberate move to deny the military any opposition figurehead. Khairallah was subsequently killed in a convenient helicopter crash in early May 1989 and replaced by General Abdul-Jabbar Shanshal, former minister of state for military affairs.

In Iran following the ceasefire there were substantial reports of rifts between the Islamic Revolutionary Guard Corps (Pasdaran) and the Iranian military. Throughout the war there had been ongoing rivalry as well as competition for resources. However, reports of attempted coups were probably a smokescreen to mask political purges carried out by the government.

The Martyrs' memorial in Baghdad, built in 1983 to commemorate Iraqi troops killed in the Iran-Iraq War. (Author's Collection)

Saddam's T-72 tank fleet steadily expanded during the war thanks to Moscow. (via Author)

Ayatollah Khomeini soon found himself at loggerheads with his acting commander-in-chief Rafsanjani. Toward the end of the conflict, with Pasdaran prestige at a low, Rafsanjani was able to bypass its commander Mushin Rezaee and its minister Mushin Rafiqdust by attempting to create a unified command structure and improving coordination with the military. Despite these moves Rafsanjani failed to integrate the regular army with the Pasdaran, a move that was naturally fiercely opposed by the radicals who feared losing their power base. Khomeini's appointment of Hajatoislam Adullah Nouri as his personal representative on the Revolutionary Guard command seemed to strip Rafsanjani's power over it.

Coup attempts mounted from within the Iranian military, based supposedly on a pro-Western network, probably represented a power shift in favour of the radicals. However, the Pasdaran was not without its dissenters. In March 1989 Mehdi Khan, commander of the IRGC 7th Vali-Asr Division, and several of his officers were shot for planning to assassinate certain leaders. Around the same time a large number of naval officers from naval headquarters in Tehran and Bandar Abbas were arrested; twenty were imprisoned while admirals Kianoosh Hakimi, Ghahreman Malekzadeh and Farhad Riahi were

Above: Iraqi BTR-60 APC. (Tom Cooper collection)

Left: Captured Iranian M60s, M47s and Scorpions on display in a park in Baghdad. (Tom Cooper collection)

A disabled Iraqi OT-64 (supplied by the Czechs or Poles to Saddam Hussein), May 1982. (Tom Cooper collection)

Iranian PoWs captured by Iraqi troops in the northern sector during the Iraqi offensive 9–14 June 1988. (*Baghdad Observer* 17/6/88 / Iraqi News Agency)

Iraqi-supported Mujahideen-e-Khalq (MEK) soldiers killed by Pasdaran troops in Kermanshah. One of the last major offensives of the war, Operation *Mersad* was a resounding victory for Iran, July 1988 (Dariush Goodarzi)

subsequently executed in April 1989. Also during March that year Khomeini's designated successor, Ayatollah Montazeri, resigned.

Upon Khomeini's death on 4 June 1989 Ali Khamenei was chosen as president and Rafsanjani remained speaker of the parliament and acting commander-in-chief of the armed forces. The purges though continued. On 17 July 1989 six senior Iranian army officers and nine Revolutionary Guard officers were reported executed for plotting to overthrow the republic, that is the rule of the ayatollahs. Those put to death included General Seyyad Shirazi, former ground forces commander, who was arrested for supporting Montazeri, and Major-General Saadi Hasani, the border forces commander. Also among the executed were four colonels, two majors and a captain.

All this reflected a deep political rift between Rafsanjani and Montazeri. The former seemed to give up the struggle and resigned as acting commander-in-chief on 2 September 1989. He informed President Khamenei that he could not fulfil his spiritual duties as well as those of acting commander-in-chief

In the wake of the Iran-Iraq War the military in both countries remained subservient to their leadership and at the same time continued to enjoy their governments' patronage. Nonetheless, numbers of war veterans did not receive the gratitude they deserved or expected. Both Iran and Iraq rapidly embarked on expensive rearmament programmes, aimed ultimately at maintaining internal as much as external security. While tensions remained, the two did not go back to war. Instead Saddam Hussein's claim on Kuwait was to spark two further wars in the region, which eventually resulted in his downfall and the collapse of Iraq.

After Iraq was removed from the international arms market in 1990, it meant that its principal suppliers were faced with the problem of trying to recover monies still owed them. For example, Iraq's outstanding debt to Russia stood at approximately $3.7 billion, most of which was believed to be for weapons. None of this though deterred continued massive arms sales to Iran and India that kept the Soviet Union's defence industries going.

Outstanding Iraqi debts to France amounted to over $8 billion, of which over $4 billion was in interest payments. Similarly, Italy was still owed $1.5 billion. The irony was that France became a victim of its own arms sales policy. Whatever commercial or strategic reasons drove Paris to support Iraq, the Iraqis' massive debts meant France could not simply walk away. France's attitude toward Iraq was tempered by its desire to be fully repaid and to gain access to Iraqi oil. France also found its support for the Iraqi air force and Iraq in general made it the target of Iranian-inspired terrorist attacks in Paris and the Lebanon.

Some might argue that the French defence industry became the victim of poetic justice. It relied heavily on exports which accounted for around 40 percent of total French arms sales. However, because of its reliance on sales to the Iraqi air force, between 1985 and 1992 the volume of French weapon exports was almost halved. Until the 1991 Gulf War Paris was able to compensate for this via increased domestic procurement, but afterward total arms sales dropped by 14 percent and continued to fall. Chinese exports also declined as a result of the end of the conflict. And shortly after the Cold War ended Moscow's and Washington's priorities in the region changed fundamentally.

A woman places flowers on the Tehran grave of an Armenian killed in action in 1988. The dates on the headstone indicate he was 19 when he died. (Hossein Zohrevand)

APPENDIX 1: IRAQI CHAIN OF COMMAND 1980–88

- Head of State, Prime Minister, CinC Armed Forces & Head of the Revolutionary Command Council: President Saddam Hussein (1979–88)
- Vice-Chairman Revolutionary Command Council, Interior Minister & Member of the Regional Command of the Ba'ath Party: Izzat Ibrahim al-Douri (dates unknown)
- Head of al-Mukhabarat (internal security agency): Barzan Ibrahim (Saddam's younger brother) (1980)
- Deputy Prime Minister, Foreign Minister, Member of the Revolutionary Command Council & Regional Command: Tariq Aziz (1980–86)
- Deputy CinC & Defence Minister: General Adnan Khairallah (1980–1988); Deputy Prime Minister & Defence Minister (1987)
- Secretary General of Defence & Adjutant Armed Forces: Sattar Ahmed Jassin (1985)
- Chief of General Staff: General Abd al-Jabar Shanshal (1984)
- Republican Guard Supervisor: General Hussein Kamel al-Majid (1982); Minister of Military Industries (1987)
- CinC Operations East of the Tigris & Adjutant Armed Forces: General Hisham Salah al-Fakhri (1984)
- CinC People's Army (Militia): Commander Taha Yassin Ramadan (1982); acting Prime Minister (1987)
- CinC Air Force: Air Marshal Hamid Sha'aban (1985)
- Naval Chief of Staff: Admiral Abelmohamed Abdallah (1984)

APPENDIX 2: IRANIAN CHAIN OF COMMAND 1980–88

- Head of the Supreme Defence Council, Supreme Religious & Political Leader (Faq'ih): Ayatollah Ruhallah Khomeini (1979–88)
- Head of State (subordinate to Supreme Head of State): President Hojatoleslam Ali Khamenei (1987)
- Prime Minister: Mir Hossein Moussavi (1987)
- Minister of Defence: Mostafa Chamran (1979–80), Colonel Javad Fakoori (1980–81), Colonel Mousa Namjoo (1981), Colonel Mohammad Salimi (1981–84), Colonel Mohammad Reza Rahimi (1984–85), Colonel Mohammad Hossein Jalali (1985–89)
- Head Joint Chiefs of Staff: General Valiollah Fallahi (1981)
- Second-in-Command Joint Chiefs of Staff: Akbar Hashemi Rafsanjani (1988)
- CinC Armed Forces: President Abolhassan Banisadr (dismissed in 1981), Mohsen Rezaie (1985)
- Armed Forces Chief of Staff: General Ghassemali Zahirnejad (1982)
- Commander of the Army & Gendarmerie: Brigadier-General Ghassemali Zahirnejad (1980)
- CinC Ground Forces: Colonel Sayyed Shirazi (1983), General Ali Sayyed Shirazi (from 1984)
- CinC Islamic Revolutionary Guard Corps: Kazam Bojnurdi (1980), Moshen Rezaee (1981)
- Operations Commander Islamic Revolutionary Guard Corps: Abu-Sharif (dates unknown)
- CinC Air Force: Colonel Javad Fakouri (1980); Major Mo'inifar (1984), Colonel Sadiri (1985?), Colonel Sadiq (1986)
- Deputy CinC Air Force: Airman Bazargan (1985), Colonel Abbas Abedini (defected to the West in 1987)
- CinC Navy: Captain Bahram Afzali (dates unknown); Darwish Amir Yeganeh (dates unknown), Mohammed Hussein Malekkzadegan (dates unknown)
- CinC Basij (Militia): Mohammad Ali Rahmani (dates unknown)

APPENDIX 3: IRAQI ORDER OF BATTLE 1983–88

The Iraqi army redeployed in 1982 with 1st Corps comprising two divisions holding the far north, 2nd Corps with ten divisions in the Baghdad area, 3rd Corps with eight divisions defending Basra and 4th Corps on the Euphrates acting as strategic reserve. These corps were soon expanded and fought on a number of different fronts.

Basra Sector: Southern Front

Major-General Maher Abd al-Rashid (1986)
Major-General Tala Khalil al-Douri, replaced by Lieutenant-General Dhiya'uldin Jamal (1987)
3rd Corps: General Hisham Salah al-Fakhri (1986)
4th Corps: General Jabbouri (1986)
7th Corps:
    2nd Infantry Division
    11th Infantry Division: Brigadier Abdul-Wahid al-Rabat (1987)
    26th Infantry Division
    28th Infantry Brigade
    704th Infantry Brigade
    5 x Presidential Guard Brigades

Ahwaz Sector: Southern Central Front

General Saadi Tooma (1983)
Major-General Maher Abd al-Rashid (1984)
3rd Corps

Dezful Sector: Central Front

General Hisham Salah al-Fakhri (1984)
General Thalit Sultan Ahmed (1985)
4th Corps:
    Saladin Armoured Division
    Special Forces Brigade*

---

* This unit along with elements of the Presidential Palace Guard was involved in taking Khorramshahr.

Mehran Sector: Northern Central Front

General Dhai' Jeyad Tawfiq (1984)

2nd Corps:

- 16th Armoured Division
- 66th Commando Brigade
- 70th Armoured Brigade
- 433rd Infantry Brigade
- 705th Infantry Brigade

Qasr-e-Shirin Sector: Northern Front

5th Corps:

- 21st Infantry Division
- 1st Commando Brigade

Mangesh Sector: Kurdish Front

General Ali Hussein al-Gowi (dates unknown)

1st Corps

5th Corps:

- 708th Infantry Brigade
- Presidential Guard Brigade
- plus forces of Patriotic Union of Kurdistan & Iranian Kurdish Democratic Party

Mobile Reserves

Armoured Corps:

- 3rd, 6th, 10th, 12th, 17th and 37th Armoured Divisions
- 1st, 5th, 14th and 51st Mechanized Divisions

Republican Guard Corps:

6–12 brigades

By the end of the war these had grown to two armoured and two mechanized divisions and three motorized infantry divisions comprising the *Hammurabi, Medina, Baghdad* and *Tawakalna* respectively and the *Adna, Al-Faw* and *Nebuchadnezzar*. There was also a Special Forces division.

Paramilitary Reserves

The People's Army (conducted rear area security and logistical support), backed by frontier guards and security troops.

APPENDIX 4: IRANIAN ORDER OF BATTLE 1983–88

The Iranian army could muster just six weak divisions in 1980, with a single armoured division in Khuzestan. As a result the poorly armed *Pasdaran* militia had to bear the brunt of the Iraqi invasion, which involved half a dozen full-strength divisions. By 1985 the *Pasdaran* had been organized into around twelve infantry divisions. The army also became a largely infantry force.

Southern Front

Islamic Revolutionary Guard Corps (Pasdaran Inqilab):

    3rd *Golden* Division

    7th *Vali-Asr* Division

    8th *Najaf-Ashraf* Division

    25th *Karbala* Division

    77th *Golden* Division*

    ? *Ashoura* Division

    5th Revolutionary *Khomeini* Guards Division

    7th Revolutionary Guards Division

    14th Revolutionary Guards Division

    25th Revolutionary Guards Division

    31st Revolutionary Guards Division

    41st Revolutionary Guards Division

    23rd Special Forces Division

    Special Martyrs' Brigade

Regular Army units:

    30th *Mazandaran* Division

    77th *Khorassan* Division*

    81st *Bakhtaran* Division

---

* Giving Revolutionary Guard and regular army divisions the same numbers must have caused confusion. The Guard ended up with about 30 divisions while the army had half this number, though both had a similar overall strength. Inevitably their respective commanders fell out over the conduct of the war. The army disliked the Guards' insistence on fighting costly and often unnecessary attritional battles. Both organizations also competed with the *Basij* Popular Mobilization Army for manpower. The latter used recruits as young as 12.

3rd Brigade

8th Brigade

19th Brigade

plus brigades from the following:

    21st Infantry Division

    28th Infantry Division

    77th Infantry Division

    92nd Armoured Division

Mehran Front

10th *Lords of the Martyrs* Revolutionary Guards Division

Kurdish/Northern Front

64th Infantry Division (Regular Army)

28th Infantry Division (Regular Army)

two other Regular Army divisions

plus units from the Islamic Revolutionary Guard Corps, Gendarmerie & Kurdish
    Democratic Party

APPENDIX 5: IRAQI AIRCRAFT IMPORTS 1977-88

Supplier	System	Ordered	Status
Argentina	20 x IA-58A Pucara light aircraft	1986	Discussions only; no aircraft ever delivered
China	4 x B-6 bombers	1985	First export of the Soviet Tu-16 copy
Egypt/Brazil	50–80 x EMB-312 Tucano trainers	1983	From Brazil & Egyptian licensed production, 50 delivered by 1987, with an option for another 30
Egypt/China	40–80 x F-7 fighters	1983	Assembled in Egypt & Jordan, delivered by 1987
Egypt	8 x Tu-16 bombers	1985?	On loan from the Egyptian Air Force, in service in Iraq in the mid-1980s
Egypt	10 x SA-342L helicopters	1987	Unconfirmed
France	40 x Mirage F-1 fighters	1977	First batch
France	100 x Gazelle, Lynx & Puma helicopters	1979	
France	29 x Mirage F-1 fighters, including 6 x trainers	1982	Second batch, delivered by 1985
France	24 x Mirage F-1C fighters	1983	All delivered by 1987
France	28 x Mirage F-1C fighters	1986	Open-ended order for attrition replacements; delivery at 2/month 12–24 on order brings total since 1979 to estimated 125–137
France	16 x Mirage F-1C fighters	1987	Delivery embargoed in 1990 following Iraq's invasion of Kuwait; in addition to 113 already ordered

France	6 x AS-332 Super Puma helicopters	1988	Status unknown, probably for the Iraqi Navy or Iraqi Army Air Corps
Germany	6 x BK-117 helicopters	1984	Delivered by 1985
Italy	2 x A-109 & 5 x AB-212 helicopters	1984	For the Iraqi Navy, embargoed due to Iran-Iraq War
North Korea	30 x F-6 fighters		Delivered 1986, unconfirmed
Spain	24 x BO-105 helicopters	1984	For the IrAAC, some equipped with SS-11 antitank missiles
Sudan	10 x MiG-21 fighters	1978	Delivered 1979, unconfirmed
Switzerland	48 x AS-202/18A trainers	1978	Delivered by 1980
Switzerland	40 x PC-7 trainers	1979	
Switzerland	31 x PC-9 trainers	1985 & 1986	Denied by manufacturer, 1st batch of 16 believed delivered in 1987
U.S.A.	45 x 214ST & 24 x 530MG helicopters	1985	Allegedly for civil use, some possibly delivered; undoubtedly used by IrAAC
U.S.S.R.	? x MiG-21/23 fighters	1977	Modernization of IrAF included listed aircraft. MiG-21s may have come from Sudan.
U.S.S.R.	150 x MiG-23/25/27 fighters, 40 x Mi-24 & ? x Mi-8 helicopters	1979	Delivered during early 1980s
U.S.S.R.	30 x Su-20 ground-attack aircraft	1983	Delivered by 1985
U.S.S.R.	50 x MiG-23BN & 30 x MiG-25 fighters	1984	Part of a $2.5bn deal; delivered by 1985
U.S.S.R.	40 x Su-25 ground-attack aircraft	1985	Delivered by 1987
U.S.S.R.	? x MiG-23BN, 45 x MiG-27, 24 x MiG-29 fighters, ? x Mi-24 helicopters	1986	Part of a $3bn deal; mostly delivered in 1987

APPENDIX 6: IRAQI AIR-TO-AIR MISSILE IMPORTS 1977–88

Supplier	System	Ordered	Status
Egypt	? x 80mm air-to-surface rockets		For MiG-21s, unconfirmed
France	267 x R-530 air-to-air missiles	1977	For F-1s, delivered by 1985
France	? x R-550 air-to-air missiles	1977	For F-1s, delivered by 1985
France	638 x AM-39 Exocet antiship missile	1983	For Super Étendards and F-1s, delivered by 1987
France	240 x AS-30L air-to-surface missile	1984	For F-1s, believed delivered by 1988, unconfirmed
France	350 x AS-30L air-to-surface missiles	1989	Included limited final assembly, status unknown
France	36 x AM-39 Exocet & 48 x AS-15TT antiship missiles	1989	For AS-332 & AS-365 helicopters respectively, status unknown
U.S.S.R.	840 x AA-2 Atoll air-to-air missiles	1975	For MiG-23s, delivered by 1985
U.S.S.R.	330 x AA-2 Atoll air-to-air missiles	1979	For MiG-21s & MiG-25s, delivered by 1985
U.S.S.R.	? x AS-4 Kitchen and AS-5 Kelt air-to-surface missiles	?	For Tu-16s & Tu-22s, delivered 1984; some may have come via Egypt
U.S.S.R.	304 x AA-8 Aphid air-to-air missiles	1985 & 1986	For MiG-29s, delivered by 1987
U.S.SR	96 x AA-7 Apex air-to-air missiles	1986	For MiG-29s, delivered 1987.
U.S.S.R.	40 x AS-14 Kedge air-to-surface missiles	1988	Delivered by 1989

APPENDIX 7: IRAQI AIR-DEFENCE MISSILE IMPORTS 1979-88

Supplier	System	Ordered	Comments
Egypt	44 x SA-6 Gainful surface to-air-missiles	1987	Unconfirmed, believed four refurbished batteries ordered
Egypt	? x Sakr Eye manportable surface-to-air missile	1987	Improved version of the Soviet SA-7, in production since 1984, unspecified number; may have also supplied Early Bird an SA-2 copy
France	150 x AMX-30 Roland air defence system plus 600–900 x missiles	1981	90 x launchers & 600 x missiles possibly delivered by 1987
France	10 x Tiger point defence radar	1987	Trailer-mounted versions supplied, some modified as airborne early warning radar; delivered 1988/9; numbers unconfirmed
Poland	200 x SA-6 missiles	1985	Unconfirmed, delivered by 1985
U.S.S.R.	52xSA-6 Gainful launchers & 520xmissiles	1979	Numbers unconfirmed, possibly all delivered by 1987
U.S.S.R.	36 x SA-8 Gecko launchers & 432 x missiles, plus 30 x SA-9 Gaskin launchers & 240 x missiles	1982	As above

APPENDIX 8: U.S. ARMS SHIPMENTS TO IRAN 1985–86

Above: Iranian F-4E Phantom II armed with an AGM-65 Maverick, takes off.

Left: Islamic Republic of Iran Air Force F-4 Phantom II refuelling through a boom during the war. (IRIAF)

1985	
July	Israeli Prime Minister Shimon Peres is told by an Israeli businessman that the U.S. and Israel should offer Iran weapons to help get American hostages in Lebanon released
Early September	Two planeloads of arms arranged by Israel arrive in Iran
13 September	508 American tube-launched, optically-tracked, wire-guided (TOW) antitank missiles arrive via Israel
18/19 December	Transport aircraft flies from Israel via Turkey to Tabriz in northern Iran with U.S. TOW antitank missiles and Hawk antiaircraft missiles
Unknown	Cargo ship departs Italy with spare parts for U.S.-built F-4 Phantom jets and U.S.-made helicopters. Arrives in Israel where parts are unloaded onto another ship at Eilat and sent to Bandar Abbas, Iran
1986	
17 January	U.S. National Security Council members John Poindexter and Oliver North memo to President Reagan refers to 'The Israeli Plan' and Israel's wish to stabilize the balance of power between Iran and Iran. The Iranians want 4,000 TOW missiles. Reagan secretly signs an order authorizing contracts with Iran and lifting the ban on some U.S. arms shipments to Iran, without notifying Congress
Mid-February	1,000 TOW antitank missiles arrive in Iran via Israel
4 July	23 tons of sophisticated spare parts for the Iranian Air Force arrive at Tehran's Mehrabad airport
17 October	Danish ship *Morso* chartered by a Swedish arms dealer takes 26 containers of 'Israeli'-produced spare parts for U.S. tanks and artillery from Eilat to Bandar Abbas.
27 October	500 TOW antitank missiles arrive in Iran via Israel
2/7 November	Despite rising U.S. public outcry, another cargo ship carries more Israeli-produced parts for U.S. military equipment to Bandar Abbas
Total Shipments: Approximately 2,000 TOW antitank and 235 Hawk antiaircraft missiles plus an unspecified amount of spare parts	
Results: During the Iranian offensive of January/February 1987 these weapons contributed to the destruction of 95 Iraqi armoured vehicles and 69 aircraft.	

BIBLIOGRAPHY

Aburish, Saïd K. *Saddam Hussein: The Politics of Revenge*. London: Bloomsbury, 2001

Azhary, M. S. El (ed.). *The Iran-Iraq War: An Historical, Economic and Political Analysis*. London: Croom Helm, 1984

Brogan, Patrick. *World Conflicts: Why and Where they are Happening*. London: Bloomsbury, 1989

Brown, Ashley & Grant, Reg (ed). *The Military Yearbook 1987*. London: Oriole, 1987

Chubin, Shahram. *Soviet Policy Towards Iran and the Gulf*. Adelphi Papers 157. London: International Institute for Strategic Studies, 1980

Collective, Khamsin. *The Gulf War: Arab Nationalism and the Palestinian Struggle*. London: Ithaca, 1986

Coughlin, Con. *Saddam: The Secret Life*. London: Macmillan, 2002

Fursdon, F. W. E. 'The Iraq/Iran War.' *Jane's 1981–82 Military Annual*. London: Jane's, 1981

Grummon, Stephen R. *The Iran-Iraq War: Islam Embattled*. The Washington Papers/92. Washington: Praeger, 1982

Heller, Mark (ed.). *The Middle East Military Balance 1984*. Tel Aviv: Jaffe Center for Strategic Studies, 1984

Hiro, Dilip. *The Longest War: The Iran-Iraq Military Conflict*. London: Grafton, 1989

Karsh, Efraim & Inari, Rautsi. *Saddam Hussein: A political Biography*. London: Futura, 1991

Karsh, Efraim. *The Iran-Iraq War 1980-1988*. Oxford: Osprey, 2002

_____. *The Iran-Iraq War: A Military Analysis*. Adelphi Papers 220. London: International Institute for Strategic Studies, 1987

King, Ralph. *The Iran-Iraq War: The Political Implications*. Adelphi Papers 219. London: International Institute for Strategic Studies, 1987

Laffin, John. *War Annual 1*. London: Brassey's Defence, 1986

Pivka, Otto von. *Armies of the Middle East*. London: Patrick Stephens, 1979

Rahman, Kanaan M. Abdul. *The Iran/Iraq War: 3,000BC–1988AD*. London: As-Sabaq, 1988

Short, Martin & McDermott, Anthony. *The Kurds*. Minority Rights Group, Report No.23. London: MRG, 1981

Stockholm International Peace Research Institute. *SIPRI Yearbook 1986: World Armaments and Disarmaments*. Oxford: Oxford University Press, 1986

Stockholm International Peace Research Institute. *SIPRI Yearbook 1988: World Armaments and Disarmaments*. Oxford: Oxford University Press, 1988

The International Institute for Strategic Studies. *The Military Balance 1980–81*. London: Arms and Armour, 1980

⸻⸻⸻⸻⸻⸻⸻⸻⸻⸻⸻⸻⸻⸻⸻⸻⸻⸻⸻⸻. *The Military Balance 1985–86*. London: IISS, 1985

⸻⸻⸻⸻⸻⸻⸻⸻⸻⸻⸻⸻⸻⸻⸻⸻⸻⸻⸻⸻. *The Military Balance 1988–89*. London: IISS, 1988*

Timmerman, Kenneth R. *The Death Lobby: How the West Armed Iraq*. London: Bantam, 1992

Trab Zemzemi, Abdel-Majid. *The Iraq-Iran War: Islam and Nationalisms*. San Clemente: United States Publishing, 1986

Periodicals

Dawisha, K. 'Moscow and the Gulf War', *The World Today*, Vol. 37 No. 1. January 1981

Derrick, J. 'U.S.A–Iran Arms Deal, Iran-Iraq: is the Military Balance Tilting?' *The Middle East*. January 1987

Desmond, E. W. 'A War Without End', *Time*. 28 July 1986

Dobson, C. 'War Flares Among the Gulf Oilfields', *Now!* 26 September–2 October 1980

Hammat, L. 'Iranian Oil for Israel', *The Middle East*. November 1982

Hargreaves, R. 'How Carter Failed to Seal the Gulf', *Now!* 3 October–9 October 1980

Johnson, M. 'Choosing Up Sides', *Time*. 20 October 1980

⸻⸻⸻ . 'The Blitz bogs Down', *Time*. 13 October 1980

Olson, W. J. 'The Iran-Iraq War and the Future of the Persian Gulf', *Military Review*. Vol. LXIV No. 3. March 1984

⸻⸻⸻ . 'The Iran-Iraq War: A Dialogue of Violence', *Defense Analysis*. Vol. 2 No. 3. September 1986

Rubinstein, A. Z. 'The U.S.SR and Khomeini Iran', *International Affairs*. Vol. 57 No. 4. August 1981

Segal, D. 'The Air War in the Persian Gulf', *Air University Review*. Vol. XXXVII No. 3. March–April 1986

Smith, W. E. 'Threats of a Wider War', *Time*. 12 March 1984

Watson R. & Sciolino E. 'Khomeini's Holy War in the Gulf', *Newsweek*. 12 March 1984

---

* The annual IISS *Strategic Survey* was also consulted.

Index

Acknowledgements

My thanks to Chris Cocks, the Cold War series commissioning editor, for instigating this project. I wrote extensively on the Iran-Iraq War during the 1980s when it was regularly overshadowed by a host of other conflicts including Afghanistan, Angola, Ethiopia, the Falklands, Lebanon and Mozambique. In particular, due to the Cold War, the Soviet military presence in Afghanistan became the main focus of world attention. Few seemed to grasp the long-term regional or religious implications of Saddam's war against the ayatollahs. In that respect thanks are also due to Anoushirvan Ehteshami, Michael Harris and Peter Moore who supported my original research this book is based on. Likewise, Henry Dodds and Tony Banks did much to encourage me on this path as a defence writer.

About the Author

Anthony Tucker-Jones is a former defence intelligence officer and a widely published expert on regional conflicts, counter-terrorism and armoured and aerial warfare. He is the author of over forty books including *The Vietnam War: The Tet Offensive 1968*, *The Gulf War: Operation Desert Storm 1990–1991*, *The Afghan War: Operation Enduring Freedom 2001–2014* and *The Iraq War: Operation Iraqi Freedom 2003–2011*. He is security and terrorism correspondent for intersec—*The Journal of International Security*. Anthony writes extensively for several Pen & Sword military history series including 'Cold War 1945–1991' and 'History of Terror'. His website can be found at www.atuckerjones.com.